Khalid bin Ali Al-Mukhaini was born in the city of Sur in the Sultanate of Oman in the year 1970. He graduated from Dartmouth Naval College in the United Kingdom in 1990. He is now a retired naval officer and is devoted to studying history in general and naval history in particular. He served as the head of Bahrona magazine, which specializes in various maritime affairs. He wrote a book entitled *The Road to Sur* in which he talks about the history of the Omani city of Sur, and he also wrote two novels entitled *Samha* in Arabic and *The Rise of the Phoenix*. Additionally, he has contributed to writing many different marine and historical articles.

Khalid Almukhaini

SAMHA

The Diary of Aqeel bin Abdullah Al-Ma'alim

AUSTIN MACAULEY PUBLISHERS™

LONDON • CAMBRIDGE • NEW YORK • SHARJAH

ISBN – 9789948792857– (Paperback)
ISBN – 9789948792864– (E-Book)

Application Number: MC-10-01-6176767
Age Classification: 13+

Printer Name: iPrint Global Ltd
Printer Address: Witchford, England

First Published 2023
AUSTIN MACAULEY PUBLISHERS FZE
Sharjah Publishing City
P.O Box [519201]
Sharjah, UAE
www.austinmacauley.ae
+971 655 95 202

Translated from Arabic by Khaula Almukhaini.

Glossary

No.	Pages	Word	Meaning
1	12	Al-Ghanja	A type of ships used for travelling long distances. It is known for its square front and pointed back.
2	12	Samha	The name of the ship. It means the easy going.
3	16	Al Jalali Fort	A big fort that is built on the top of a mountain at the entrance of Mutrah port in Muscat. It was used as a jail at that time.
4	18	Al Farda	It is a place in which the traders pay the taxes for the government. It is usually situated in the area of the port where all the ships stack the goods.
5	23	Diwan	A classic Arabic word that means a book.
6	23	Abu Tayyib Al Mutanabbi	A famous classic poet who lived hundreds of years ago.

7	24	Al Alam Palace	The Flag Palace is the official residence for the Sultan of Oman. It is situated on the Oman Gulf in Muscat.
8	24	Sanqur sweet	Sanqur is the name of the trader who used to sell the traditional Omani sweet at that time.
9	27	AL-Tha'alibi	A famous Arab philosopher who specialized in the Arabic language and history.
10	27	tandoor	Traditional oven that is usually made in the shape of a cylinder. It is used to bake bread.
11	28	boom	A type of ships that is used to travel and has pointed ends from both sides. Unlike the Ghanja used in Sur which has one pointed side and one wide side.
12	36	Al-Jazer	A small coastal town in the middle of Oman.
13	42	Tayba	Another name for the City of Al Madinah Al

			Monawarah in Saudi Arabia where the Prophet Mohammed lived and died.
14	43	Al Serkal	This is the name used to call big houses in Sur. Such houses are usually owned by the owners of the ships and the rich people. The extended family of the owner lives there.
15	45	dishdasha	The white long dress worn by Omani men. Men from Sur wear the same dress but it is distinguished with colorful hand embroidery.
16	47	Al-Mutanabbi	A famous Arabic poet who lived hundreds of years ago.
17	47	Antarah bin Shaddad	A famous Arabic poet and warrior who lived in the era before Islam.
18	70	Barzat	A name used for the place where men gather and chat on different aspects of live

			on daily basis.
19	77	Imam Al-Shafi'i	A Muslim Philosopher and religious scholar.
20	42	Al Jazer	A small coastal village in the middle of Oman.
21	90	Juz Amma	The last chapter of the Holy Quran
22	12	Darbat al'liklil	It is a time of the year that comes with Stormy winds during the period of May 19 to May 30 every year. Sailors usually don't sail during this period of time.
23	96	Al-Siridan	The ship's kitchen.
24	97	Ghubat Ash Shuwaymiyyah	Ash Shuwaymiyyah is a small village on the coast in the southern part of Oman. Ghubat Ask Shuwaymiyyah is the coastal area opposite the village. It is known for the changing weather and the strong winds.
25	99	Saeed bin Wazir	A well-known poet from Sur.
26	12	Sinyyar	When two ships travel together.

27	105	Al-Hawqala	a prayer that is said at the time of fear and helplessness
28	106	Ayatul-kursi	The verse of the throne (a verse from the Holy Quran that is read at the time of fear.)
29	107	dhikr	Prayers to calm himself.
30	114	Baa'a	A unit used to measure length and one Baa'a is equal to 1.895 meters.
31	118	Thumrait	A town in the southern of Oman near Salalah.
32	120	Eid al-Adha	A religious celebration for the Muslims in which they do the Haj (visiting the holy places in Macca) and sacrifice animals (goat, sheep, camel or cow).

Introduction

Samha was one of the ships in the Suri-Omani traditional fleet from al-Ghanja. She was the pride and joy of that fleet as it included on her deck the best crew of sailors that could possibly gather on one ship.

The ship left Sur port in August of the year 1958 at the beginning of the usual annual travel season heading toward Basrah, Iraq then to India. It concluded its annual journey at the start of 1959 heading toward East Africa after many events that occurred while heading there.

For some reason, the ship was late in her journey back to Oman where it was the last ship to leave Zanzibar with another one that accompanied her half of the way back, which is an old tradition where a ship must be accompanied by another, known locally as 'Sinyyar'.

In the month of May 1959, while approaching the central region of Oman, Samha entered the area of a massive tropical cyclone that suddenly struck the Arabian Sea, under what is called locally as Darbat al'Iiklil, in which many ships were lost, the most prominent of which was Samha and 141 sailors and passengers on its board.

21ˢᵗ of Rajab 1378 AH (January 30, 1959)

With my diary tucked under my arm, I stood upon the shore of Khor Al-Batah watching the various ships that concluded the season of Basra and India and were now beginning their journey to East Africa to round off the annual sailing season in Sur.

This side of town was blessed with a wide creek which made it the ideal place to build and maintain ships during the period of low tides as the water draws back completely from it. Like a legendary dragon with tight jaws, the creek was serpent like with adequate width to include hundreds of ships within it. It kept the Suri people from having to build berms to stop the winds and helped keep the ships in a safe harbor. There is no doubt that Sur has been blessed with the creek.

I was thoroughly blinded to that beauty; too immersed in my education, I lost the joy of life. The monotony of life erased the details out of my mind… Many of the details…

Ships in various sizes and types, agile sailors moving around the place, children playing, and caravans unpacking their loads were normal daily activities. Suddenly, I was taken by the splendor of the shops that had just opened and those were among my destinations in my childhood. A sea of emotions swirled inside me thinking of how I spent my life trapped in small classrooms. Torn between looking at the sailors and listening to their chants, and remembering the dim singing voices of songs that I used to hear through my window, a room that I no longer know if I reside in or if it resides within me.

Which ship will I choose for my first trip to East Africa? It seems hard to decide since each ship has its own special features; only the sailors and the captain make a difference. How will I be able to know what is the most suitable from what I see? I, for one, have never left al-Najah School even for a day, neither as a student nor as a teacher.

"Hey you, young man! Hold the rope tight and tie it around the mooring on the quay."

The voice interrupted my thoughts. I moved instantly, quickly tying the front rope of the ship. An invisible rope linked us at that moment. I did not recognize if I was tying the rope or if it was tying me down. As the ship approached the wooden quay to dock, the rope that linked us strengthened, pulling me near and pulling the ship to me. That is the one! Did I choose the ship or did she choose me? The question settles in my mind for me to answer but only 'chance' will know how to decipher this destiny for it is its messenger.

The ship tied me to her and she is my anchor. Coxswain Ali jumped off her (or off me) and introduced himself. I asked him about departure time and he told me that it would be in two days from now. "The Al-Ghanja Samha is preparing to travel to East Africa," he continued.

He studied the features of my face trying to read its details but he quickly gave up saying, "Hungry for knowledge? We will take you with us to the north of the Arab Gulf the next season. The season of Basra for this year has passed. It will not cost you a lot, just come back next year, and take off your fancy clothes. You are in Samha, the one painted in fish oil, which knows no difference between ragged and new clothes."

"I intend to travel with you to East Africa this season."

"A tourist! Not a merchant. Anyway, I will ask the ship captain if you are serious about it."

"I am serious. I will wait for your answer."

Coxswain was gone for a while then he called from the top of the boat, "Get in, the ship captain wants to talk to you."

I climbed up slowly and with each step, Samha boarded me as well. I tried to maneuver around the stacked goods on the deck as Samha tried to overlook the monotony contorted in my spirit until I reached where the ship captain stood with the coxswain who laughed loudly.

"Did I not tell you that your new clothes cannot handle sailing in wooden ships?" he said.

I looked down at my clothes. There was a big spot of grime mixed with fish oil on its fringes. I did not find it in me to care, what would the coxswain say if he was able to see the rusty dreams that stained my soul? I looked again down at my dress and I did not care.

The ship captain was older and more reserved than coxswain was. The time could erase all but can't reach beauty nor tamper with it, and salt as well knows how to deepen suffering in faces and how to upkeep beauty until it is forever imprinted, just like it upkeeps things for ages. I looked down at my clothes and I did not care.

"Are you Aqeel bin Abdullah the assistant teacher in al-Najah School?"

The question was thrown at Aqeel but his eyes remained in another realm, like a bullet shot in the sky instead of a net thrown with patience until it is full.

"I am."

"Why do you want to travel to East Africa, son? Why leave the school when your uncle is elderly and needs your aid to manage it?"

"I got my uncle's permission to travel there until the school is reconstructed."

"You are welcome with us, son. We will be leaving in two days."

He then turned to the coxswain and said, "Take care of the young man and show him the ship and the crew after we set sail." He instructed, "We will see you in two days God willing."

He was watching a boy standing near the ship, then asked Ali about him as he seemed interested in him. Clothes seemed to be wearing down a body and a defeat that extinguished the fire in his eyes.

"The son of the merchant Saleh bin Jumaa, he was bankrupted and imprisoned in Kut Al Jalali (Al Jalali Fort) a few months ago. He had bought a ship that contained all that he owns but it burnt down with all of its content because of a load of kerosene containers. It was a real tragedy. It exploded with everyone on it in Musandam after one of the sailors snuck a smoke despite Jumaa's strict orders that no one smokes on board throughout the short trip from Dubai to Muscat.

"A horrific explosion lit up the sky above the area full of ships at dawn. He and some of his sailors miraculously survived after been thrown off the ship since they were at the back of it. The force of the blast attracted some fishermen from the Shihuh tribe, and they rushed to rescue them."

"Those who listen intently to the sea and seek the stars for guidance, know how to hear others even they already know of the truth."

"This is how I heard of it from him." Ali was then encouraged to complete. "He was unable to pay the remaining amount to the ship owner so he was then thrown in Kut Al Jalali. Many of the people sympathized with him, and sums were collected for him to release him from prison, but it was not enough, so he was sentenced three months ago to one year in prison."

23rd of Rajab 1378 AH (February 1, 1959)

Sailing from the City of Sur with the Ship Captain Nasser Bin Saif

Countless caravans piled up goods at Al Farda area until the ship captain authorizes loading them on the ship when it is ready. Despite the large number of stacks, they are never mixed up as each crew knows their goods.

During the past two days, large quantities of supplies that were piled on the coast were loaded on the ship. The ship was ready to sail after loading and the chanter began singing sea chants heralding the lifting of the anchor. His voice was raised as he sang the sailors' song:

Wa seteen ha baisa Ma jmalun hali Ashri behn kiswa Wala qut li e'alli (Sixty cents I own The joy one can feel To spend them on a gown Or buy my kids a meal)

Aqeel shivered at the eloquence of the words despite its simplicity. It has summarized the struggles of sailors and bared the reality of the temporary separation between spouses. A separation sealed by the sea, waves, sails, and wind. The farther the distance, the longer the yarn. The scent of those who are away still lingers on clothes that mothers, wives, and children smell. Each day that passes increases the hope that the sea will bring enough to support the children.

Mothers are often left with little more than sixty silver piasters for a whole year. They always wonder if the money left will be enough to support them and their children until the fathers return.

The shoreline is crowded with the sailor's wives and children in their frilly clothes along with old ship captains and sailors, while the rest of the city's men are traveling on their ships scattered in every direction. The ship's captain, brought on a large boat paddled by eight sailors, arrived in the afternoon and was the last passenger.

It is customary that the ship captains' wives do not say their farewells at the shore, but they say goodbye at the doorsteps. It appears that this custom delineates imaginary borders of the ember of separation for the ship captains from their wives and children. Borders that will be on land only because the sea will extinguish it, the land will preserve it, and the wind will fuel it further and will carry it to the sailors in the middle of the sea, so they remember that they have loved ones who they must return to.

Raising the biggest of the sails, we started our journey toward Muscat. Our first day is heavier than a body exhausted by the preparation for the first launch, heavier than even thinking about it. Our first day starts with tiredness and ends with leaving loved ones, with chests full of sorrow beforehand thinking of murky nights, in which there is neither a child nor a spouse. The sailors' chests and minds are heavy with a blue sea that will stand between them and their loved ones for long months.

Melancholic and honest are these moments and all the fake smiles these men put up melt away like a candle once they turn to the great blue. They busy themselves with work on the deck stealing last glances at loved ones whose arms turned into shades of bodies. How would the hands that embrace their beloveds bear all these farewells? Scattered eyes of wives and children that one could think they are looking at Samha and those boarding it but the sadness has settled in the heart of wives long before it. They have become accustomed to solitude and have become filled with it days before the departure. A departure they wished would be before sunset so that the darkness will swallow tears and it seems that night will cool down an ember that will only scorch up with flame at every new dawn.

On my first trip, no one came to say goodbye. I did not have a wife that I will knit a gown of patience for. I bid my parents farewell similar to the daily one I said when I headed toward al-Najah School. As if I was born on the deck of Samha, no one accompanied me. I was the happiest and most eager to see Muscat before heading to Zanzibar, although the sorrows that filled the ship made me deeply saddened, as the moments harsh in the heart of the sailors would not have passed me peacefully.

Wa seteen ha baisa Ma ajmalun hali Ashri behn kiswa
Wala qut li e'alli (Sixty cents I own The joy one can feel to
spend them on a gown Or buy my kids a meal)

I sat in a circle after dinner with some travelers and crewmembers to converse as we near the ancient city of Qalhat. One of the sailors wondered aloud about stories about the city so another one answered, "I heard from my grandfather that the reason that the city was destroyed is that a man who resided in it had a beautiful and lonely daughter.

All the men in the city adored her but her father deemed them all unworthy of her. They asked her father for her hand in marriage repeatedly until he grew tired of them. The father then went to the city judge to complain, 'I have one palm tree that people ask me for, do I keep it or give it to them.' The judge is unaware of the matter ruled based on what was said; commanding the father to keep the tree as he is entitled to it. One night, while his daughter was sleeping, her father was enticed with her and he violated her. The abused girl spent the night cursing her father, the judge, and the entire city, and the wrath of God struck the city, so the city was flooded with water to cleanse the earth from the defilement of mankind."

"It is a myth! I said. "How do you expect me to explain a myth?" I said to myself.

"Since the beginning of time, people tend to justify natural phenomena which the mind is unable to find a logical reason for with stories fabricated by imagination. It then integrates itself into the folklore, and we call them a myth. An earthquake occurred about five hundred years ago that was so powerful that it buried the greater part of Qalhat city to the sea; this is how it was mentioned in history books. Later, the Portuguese (Albuquerque) cannons destroyed what was left of it, except for a building called (Bibi Mariam). It eluded their cannons so it remained standing to this date."

The coxswain enthusiastically told me, "They say that beneath its gate is a great treasure, Aqeel!"
"It might be; I have never heard of that."

"No one can enter any of the sealed cave unless they repeat the saying 'Salem bin Salim bin Suwailem' throughout their way in, so they will not be abducted by Jinn, after breaking the seal of the curse off the cave."

"It is easy enough to say. But how to break the seal?" "One must slaughter a spotted hyena at the gate, according to one of the elderlies."

"It is worth a try," I replied with a laugh.

"Definitely!" he responded with glee. "It seems like it would be a pleasant and quick trip with you onboard, Aqeel." We continued on our way to Quriyat, where we laid down until dawn.

Neither of them knew then that destiny was laying down its tale, just as if we were devouring the tales to kill time. In vain, we thought that it will pass, but it was weaving a garment with three invisible needles. One of trickery, the second of brilliance, and the third of patience. It will be worn by other people in another time not so far away.

24th of Rajab 1378 AH (February 2, 1959)

At dawn, we were alongside Abu Dawud's head. We raised the anchor and moved slowly with the early morning breeze; a morning that is heavier than Samha.

After first light, I joined the sailors who were drinking coffee, and they take the initiative to ask me about the first night at sea. I told them that I slept fairly well but was interrupted by the movement of the sailors and their voices as they changed their night shifts.

I am dying to see the long-standing capital, which we will reach in the afternoon.

The light breeze of the morning did not move the heavy body of the ship as expected.

The large sail was not fully filled, so the ship's captain ordered to turn on the ship's engine. Its noise interrupted the wonderful morning silence, while the sailors quickly folded the sails happily as the engine will relieve them from working for some time.

I headed to the stern of the ship where the captain (Al Nokhodha) and the Coxswain (Al-Majdami) were talking, and they asked me to sit with them.

I liked that the captain, Nasser, held Diwan of Abu Tayyib Al Mutanabbi.

He surprised me with an unexpected question: "Do you memorize any poetry?"

"I memorize a lot of it."

The coxswain Ali asked me to recite something of Hafiz Al Maskari poetry and I hesitated because what I meant was classic poetry and not folk poetry. I then recited his poem in which he says,

To turn back time, to be unbound from this wooden fate In a house of mine drinking the colocynth I cultivate Leaving all behind, still wholly adorned

If the coasts from my side strayed

Once abandoned, they called, "Come near." The old days serene me, toward it I steer When fate has fallen, and my legs gave out "Hafiz has deserted us and left," they shout Hafiz has relinquished and the hope forgo His kids, home, and the doctrine he threw

They were delighted when they heard the droll poem and then the captain brought a bowl of porridge with ghee to honor me with it, and I had it with a cup of coffee with cardamom.

The ship captain liked the poem, saying: It was a good choice, it is one of my favorite poetry. I told him that I only memorized this poem, then we all laughed.

"Tell me about the city of Muscat?" I asked them.

"Do not be in a hurry; you will see its market Sidab and its mountain pass, the forts of Muscat, and Al Alam Palace. You will eat the famous (Sanqur) sweets if you like and you will see the gate of Muscat and the different types of people therein."

"However, we will not stay more than two days, we want to quickly take the cargo of dates and leave, hoping to find Nabhan bin Salem, the merchant, has prepared the cargo in the port of Muscat as he promised us. There is no time to waste waiting as we will be two days behind the rest of the ships that have preceded us to Zanzibar."

That morning, I met the ship's carpenter, an elderly man. I found him working on a wooden window and greeted him. He looked at me and asked me a lot of questions without stopping.

He did not return the salutation, but he asked million questions, bowing his head and busy with his window, I think the answers do not mean anything to him.
"Tell me what brought you, son?"

"Is the earth, despite its vastness, seemed to close in on you? Or is it pure curiosity that got into you as you watched our ships sail and disappear behind the horizon?"

"Or are you one of the men who escape from their responsibilities in order to be liberated?"

I know that sailing itself is an adventure. Only a brave man who is earnestly desirous for a better tomorrow, and this better tomorrow is rarely easier than his day and yesterday. And he may make him fall into the issues of which he is indispensable, although he used the third person pronoun but I was the intended by his words. Then, still working on his wooden window, he says,

"Sit down, what's your name? I can no longer keep my head up, and I am sure that the renegades' sailors have hinted to you that I am talkative, idiots. Who does not realize that he who deals with so much damp wood and for long hours in which the marriage of silence and patience is held, is a human being who needs to talk."

He barely gave me a chance to say few words, looking delusional as no one told me about him, some letters falling out during his quick speech, good health, clear eyes and wisdom that he derived from the inspiration of wood.

We sailed slowly toward the port of Muscat, a port that resembles a horseshoe, on the left side a solid mountain bearing the Jalali Fort on its head, while the famous (Al Mirani) fort confronted us, Al Alam Palace, the Palace of the Sultan, and Al Fardha where we will register our cargo. There, I conjured history as a witness of our ancestors facing the Portuguese's cannons with their simple rifles before the liberation, after which they set out to travel through the seas conquering.

The crew dispersed shortly after finishing their lunch. Everyone had taken a side of the ship watching the port in which the movement began to be active. Sea gulls settled at the port flying over the ship, the dark mountains seemed to dominate the scene like stakes of determination and steadfastness embracing the comers and warning them at the same time. The color of the sun gave the mountains an annoying shine to the eye, which was increased by the rising humidity and temperature.

The port contains old wooden ships that look so worn out, a sight that my eyes were not familiar with.

In Sur, the ships like brides are taken care of, not getting old. No wonder, we have the best shipbuilders in Oman, and Muscat is far away, they cannot maintain their ships as Suri ship owners do.

Sur is a friendly welcoming city; this is how I think of it. Pronouncing the word is enough to take me to the eternal amazement as a child, wondering how wood would become a ship carrying people far away so we all grow except for the Indian teak wood. Regardless of the impact of the sun and the sea on its bodies, the hands of the Suri people know how to change the pale beauty to sparkle.

I spotted a military ship near Al Alam Palace and was later informed that it belonged to the British fleet which was on a visit to Muscat.

Samha found a place for her in the port between two wooden ships, where she laid her anchorage there. One of the sailors told me that the wooden ships had to lay down their anchorages and use their long boats called mashwat to move and load goods.

Soon, the sailors were ready to spread to the external Muscat market, to meet with other sailors from Sur who had arrived before us, to buy Muscat sweets as well, and to eat meals different from the meals they were accustomed to during the past two days.

The Coxswain stopped them, saying:

"None of you will move until you finish all the work."

He said it after seeing the cargo piled up in a side close to customs, with its owner who was waiting. It took three hours until the shipment of dates stowed away in a way that satisfied the Coxswain, and then he authorized everyone to leave after that.

"You are allowed to leave now."

The sailors left the ship that night except for the alternates. I bought myself some sweets and biscuits, and a philology book for Al-Tha'alibi from Mulla Ali bookshop in the market.

I did not forget to buy some hot tandoor bread for the old, talkative carpenter, my companion during my long journey. I am happy to know him as you never get bored sitting with such a person.

I wandered around the many diverse shops and stores. The wool products of the Bedouin women are incomparable to anything else. The weapons shop amazed me with the diversity of guns therein. I had never seen anything similar to them before. It was an opportunity for me to visit the barbershop as well, as the journey is long and the water for bathing in the ship is very little.

The ships of Sur are the most numerous in the port. I saw Iranian sailors on the roof of their big boom and a Kuwaiti ship of which its sailors gathered in a café drinking tea with local sweet bread, then I saw them heading to the sweet shop that I had previously bought from.

The sunset cast a shadow over the large castle overlooking the port and the movement dimmed in the area. I headed to our ship's boat, and found some sailors waiting for the number to be completed to bring us back to the ship. The ship's captain and Ali preceded me to it, and the cook had finished preparing dinner for the crew.

My first visit has ended… Muscat, crowded with coherent people despite the misery engraved on the wrinkles of the faces of some of them; misery is self-evident… Muscat with its brown guardian mountains, free airspace, multiple faces, and various dialects, the scent of a real history, even if it appears to me pale and short of its historical role, which it played during its maritime glory. Muscat is more like a hag out of time attempting to hide her shattered pieces while her soul is still alive and young, hoping for a chance to be born again.

25th of Rajab 1378 AH (February 3, 1959)

The next morning someone came to tell me that the ship captain was waiting for me at the sidewalk. I went quickly and found him with Ali. They were elegant, wearing daggers, and holding their sticks. The ship captain draped his turban in bright colors on his shoulder, as is the custom of our elders.

"You will go with us," Coxswain said.

"Give me more time to change my clothes; your looks indicate that it is an important visit."

We approached the Al Alam Palace area in Muscat. I saw guards and people from different backgrounds and I asked Ali, "Who will we meet?"

"Sayyid Shihab bin Faisal, the Sultan's deputy here."

We entered the council, which was crowded with notables and tribal chiefs. We greeted all the attendees, one by one, as usual. I was surprised by the numbers of the notables the ship captain knew, one of them came taking his hand to sit near Sayyid Shihab. After drinking coffee, the ship captain spoke words that I did not understand due to the distance between us. He then took out a purse of silver piasters from Maria Theresa's riyals, which were taken by the guards. He then called upon the clerk who wrote something that he gave to

Sayyid Shihab to sign and stamp and then delivered it to the guard. The ship captain stood up and left the council. We followed him and I asked Ali, "What has just happened?"

"Jumah bin Saleh has been released."

"The boy's father who was miserable near the ship on the morning of our departure from Sur?"

The ship captain turned to me and said, "We would not leave one of the men of Sur in prison and we could get him out. Jumah will have lunch with us today, then we will send him to Sur in one of the small ships heading there carrying the sweet of Muscat to his family."

My respect for the captain grew after this incident, and I realized the reason behind his good reputation and the love of his crew for him. This incident brought back to me the feeling I got when I held Samha's rope to tie it to the anchorage, I may have begun to understand the secret of this attraction.

26th of Rajab 1378 AH (February 4, 1959)

"Where did he go?"

"Look for the miserable Obaid," he shouted to the sailors who were still searching for the sailor Obaid in the ship and the areas near the port.

Coxswain flared up as the time to inform the ship captain that the number is completed approached. It is a customary practice before untying the ropes from the dock and start sailing.

"We'll be late… Where did he disappear?"

He saw me and rushed to me, asking, "Didn't he tell you anything last night?"

"You were both talking before I went to sleep."

"He did not say that he would go anywhere but was complaining about the conditions prevailing in Sur. He seemed confused and distracted during his speech as if he was justifying something he had done or would do. I did not say anything. He was asking and answering himself, I was just listening. He talked about the conditions of his family in Sur, various matters that mostly feed into the racism of society. He was indignant to the point that he said a word that I did not understand, but I felt sorry for him, so I did not ask him."

"What did he say?" Ali asked me anxiously.

"Al-Balooz! He said he will go to Al-Balooz, he did not tell me when, where, or who is Al-Balooz. It was late, and I couldn't help or talk to him for a long time."

I did not need to ask about the meaning of the word, for it seemed to have a direct effect on Ali's face at the same moment I finished pronouncing the word. He then ran quickly toward the ship captain, who quickly wore his turban, and both rushed out of the ship.

I was curious about the significance of the term, so I asked the carpenter Farhan about it. He said laughing, "The son of Salma did it," then followed that with a loud laugh.

I asked him what he meant; I didn't understand what was happening.

"Obaid freed himself from slavery." "How's that? Is he a slave to anyone at all?"

The sailor Obaid is from the last families that are still under slavery. All slaves were liberated a hundred years ago by an initiative of the people of Sur. The slave trade was officially prohibited forty years before that. In Sur, they owned private homes and real estate, especially the owners of shipbuilding workshops. But some families remained in their old condition due to the conditions of women who did not have a breadwinner. They were married while the head of the family kept the document of slavery so that the women wouldn't be dispersed in case they were divorced and they would be left without a breadwinner.

"Then, what's Al-Balooz?"
"It is the name we use for the British Consulate in Muscat. Whoever wants to liberate himself must hold the flagpole of the British state in front of the consulate, and then he is given an official certified paper proving that he is a free person and no one has authority over him except the authority of the government whose law applies to everyone. Obaid the son of

Salma did it after complaining about his condition, he must have planned this before leaving Sur," Farhan said.

Farhan followed that with a loud laugh that had a hidden meaning, he is black but a free man.

Three whole hours passed before the ship captain and the coxswain Ali returned. He did not speak to anyone. The ship captain ordered the coxswain to raise the anchor and to sail immediately.

After that, we knew that the sailor Obaid freed himself and went to Sur carrying his freedom document with him. What audacity, if I were in his place, I might have done the same thing. What is life without freedom? I asked myself, "What will he do now?" I did not answer and I did not know why the words of that writer floated on the surface of my memory with his famous saying, "You must die every day, be born every day, and reject what you have every day. The great virtue is not in being free, but in striving for freedom. Do not be humble and ask will we win? Will we be defeated? Rather, fight and in every moment of your life make the adventure of the world your adventure." Yes, perhaps Obaid was rejected, died and was born, and everyone was away from him, even Farhan. His laughter that had a hidden meaning behind it, the most who enslave a slave is a slave like him but was given his freedom…

Obaid's incident was the talk of our evening that night. I didn't see any signs of discomfort on the captain, but Ali looked very annoyed. I guessed it was due to losing a good sailor from the crew as he had told me before that Obaid was the best steersman in Sur.

We left the port a little before sunset, Samha headed toward the Al Khiran area in Muscat, where it dropped its anchor. I did not understand why we sailed for only one hour. I said to myself that what Obaid did this morning had exhausted them and they were no longer able to continue. Because today is heavier than Samha for those who are used to monotony and the hours and days similarity like me, I went to bed early.

I was so tired I didn't know if what I heard was true. It was midnight and there was a disturbance that I didn't pay attention to at first. The truth was I wasn't sure that I was out of a dream as the voices grew louder and closer to me, making me more certain. I then got up with difficulty to see the sailors carrying rectangular dark green wooden boxes from a large wooden boat adjacent to our ship. The crew was busy and working hard, the captain himself urging them to finish quickly.

Then two men boarded the ship and talked a little. The captain gave them money and they quickly left. After that, the anchor was raised, and we continued our way toward our destination. I could not sleep after that, I prayed and waited for dawn. I was busy thinking about that suspicious load and I haven't asked anyone about it yet. But it must be smuggled, there is no other reason not to ship it from the port. Why was that suspicious time and hidden spot chosen to load it?

1ˢᵗ of Sha'ban 1378 AH (February 8, 1959)

Four days into the journey to East Africa, we were still in the central region of Oman. Wide sea, bright sky, and sailors who were killing time by singing sea chants. I was extremely bored after a couple of days of travel. The ship was slow moving and the distance was still farfetched and I have not witnessed any actual excitement. Most of my time I spent with Farhan who continued chattering while working without looking at me. Regardless of that, I liked how he talked. He seemed hardworking despite his old age; his fighting spirit is what gave him that strength.

One evening, he spoke of himself, "The idea of building a small shipbuilding workshop for my family never left my thoughts. I was captivated, obsessed with it since it meant that my family and I would leap high to settle in the clouds where the wealthy sat comfortably. Clouds that would not only rain money, but would preserve damned social classes like it is forever engraved on our skins as if we are from another species. How could one escape this really? I have been an independent carpenter who is always moving from one ship to another seasonally for a long time. Oh how do I dream of creating a magnificent ship for my own.

"Thirty years ago, I received from my mother's uncle, Saleh the skilled carpenter, a carpentry kit as a gift. The tradition adapted in Sur is that the students who master the craft are given that large bag full of primitive carpentry kit as a graduation certificate. This was in a way a recognition of their skills and providing them with the choice to work for a fixed wage for the chief carpenter or to work on their own for whomever they want. This only after they have worked in the beginning for simple meals provided to them in exchange for being taught the craft."

The anchor dropped near a small creek in the Omani region of Al-Jazer to take cover from the waves. Groups of fishermen come and go, loading the dates and trade it with fish. How wondrous are those traveling Bedouins. They mixed the Bedouin lifestyle with the sea and became skilled fishermen who maintained their camels and their Bedouin life at the same time. They did this without underestimating one lifestyle to the other. How marvelous are they? Are they actual Bedouins?

What has forced them to take on two opposing jobs between the sea and the desert? How can a person wear two skins at the same time? Fish and camels, how ironic. Is it the cruel nature that imposes its control on humans and minimizes their choices?

I asked Ali how to know the depth and the type of bottom the anchor would rest on because the anchor might be stuck in the rocks, which could make it hard to retrieve. He told me that they use Al-Belid, which is a rope with lead on its end and it has certain marks that easily determine the depth. They also place a piece of grease at its end so they can know if the bottom is suitable for throwing the anchor, or it is of the rocky type that is not suitable, according to the marine soil sample that gets attached to the piece of grease.

Ali asked some of his sailors to get ready to bring in the

salt. I asked him if I could go with them and then we waited in a boat next to the ship. The ship captain went down with us and then we were handed over tens of empty sacks and some scoops to use for filling it with salt. The sailors took a turn to the nearby village; each of us is rowing in their own wide sea. They row in the sea and I row in the fields of my memory. If it was not for education, we would have shared the same fate. Hard and enjoyable work, at least for me, I am still young when it came to the sea and I only look at things with the fascination of the first time. A passion to be open for other worlds floating on the face of memories that only engrave stereotypical images within it, of monotonous daily routine that is integrated with fulfillment. Are they truly fulfilled, or do they look at me lamenting their lack of education? Do they know that experience makes what no knowledge or science can make? Where their skins are the books, the sun is their pen and ink, and the salt is the quill.

A wasteland of salt with many small-scaled pyramids stacked as far as the eye can see. In a small bay, facing them were many poles with ropes tied to their tops and with slices of dried fish hanging from them. We went to where a man worked. Exhausted by the work, salt burned his eyes and cracked his hands. We greeted him, and the ship captain introduced himself.

The man did not pay much attention to us. He was extremely tall with big hands despite how slim he stood. His eyes were clearly protruding and his teeth were bright white. "I have to provide food for my children."
As if he was implying that, he wants money in exchange for his salt. The men looked at him with astonishment that I did not comprehend; I looked at the ship captain who did not even

flinch but he put his hand in his pocket and gave him some silver piasters. I followed the men afterward to load the salt and left him gleeful with the money he had made.

The ship captain explained to me that the tribal traditions state that one shall not take money in exchange for any amount of salt the ship-owner requests if they and the salt owner were from the same tribe or had prior blood-pact.

He followed up. "Otherwise it is insulting for those asking for money, an insult that they carry forever. This man is from the ship captain's tribe whom many of its people reside here. The ships' captains willingly compensated them with dates equivalent to the value of salt."

"May God ends the need that robs people out of their honorable qualities one by one," the ship captain added.

While we were gathered for dinner that night eating rice with roasted mutton that we have bought from the village, we saw the salt seller boarding the ship. He was focusing his eyes on the ship captain who quickly got to his feet. Confused at his appearance, they stood at the back of the ship and the latter asked him what he needs in a voice just as boisterous as he appeared. He informed the ship captain of his need for a fishing net with all of its accessories, confessing that the money is in his wife's hands and there is no possibility that he could take it back. He promised to pay back the costs of what he bought as soon as possible.

The ship captain smiled. "Is that all?" he said. "I imagined that it is an important matter, come now to dine with us!"

However, he declined and left thankful after the ship captain has ordered the coxswain to provide him with what he needs.

The next morning, while the crew was getting ready to pull up the anchor to leave, the man approached again in his big boat waving his paddles nearing the ship. He stood in his boat with his head barely reaching us, I have never seen a taller man, he asked the sailors to pull up the fish he brought in his boat, then he boarded the ship with his clothes stained in fish blood.

He sat, then he spoke. "My name is Mubarak. In addition to working in the salt ponds, I also work as a fisherman. Salt is cheap and could hardly satisfy our needs, although little they are. We are not like you sailors, traveling all around and selling everything. We live and die among the white of the salt ponds and the red of the pooling blood of the fish everywhere.

"The night you arrived, I headed to the storage, my biggest secret, the permeant solution for my financial troubles, a remote place full of fish that I have found a long time ago and that is how I named it, and it rightfully named so. Truly storage that never was less than generous, providing me with all that my heart desired of fish. However, nothing is ever perfect in this life brothers! I always struggle to reach it. I am always beat rowing back for twenty miles. None of the fishermen dared to follow me that far, although their curiosity was eating them inside out.

"I threw my net and took a nap, drained after loading salt and rowing, feeling hollowed by hunger and cold by the wind. I only was awakened by the crashing of my boat into a sand cape that was into the sea. I have no idea of how I reached there. My net was two hundred meters away from me and the boat drifted toward it quickly. I tried to pull out my net to see what was in it and it was incredibly heavy. I was unable to hurl it up at all. It was stuck in the rock! *What to do?* I wondered.

"How will I be able to find a new net with its accessories? We buy all that we need from ship owners and there is not but your ship here. Do I return what I took from the ship captain in the evening the next morning? How to do so and my wife has taken all of the money? Hell will freeze before she will give me any of it as it was her chance to buy what she and her daughters want. I was the most embarrassed due to the generosity of your gifts. If the matter happened to someone else, he would have exposed my ill-doing everywhere so it was inevitable that I would come to you.

"I was twice as embarrassed by you captain when you gave me the net and all the accessories of rope, strings, lead, and cork. I spent half a day preparing the net then I headed to my secret place which did not disappoint me this time. My boat was soon filled with fish, so I folded my net and quickly rowed toward you fearing that you have left before I reach you. Please, could you ask the sailors to pull up all of the fish now in exchange for the net?"

At first, the ship captain refused Mubarak's offer. Telling him that the net price is so much less than the amount of fish he brought, he then agreed after great effort and insistence from Mubarak. My previous judgment toward him drastically shifted after hearing his story, he was much simpler than I have first seen and only his need is what pushed him to ask for few piasters.

He excused himself but the ship captain asked him to remain for a bit then ordered the coxswain to lower a month's load of supplies as a gift from him in his boat which Mubarak accepted happily without much of argument this time. Then, after he saw the qualities of the ship captain, he turned to him and asked him to allow him to travel to Zanzibar with a load of a thousand bags of salt, and promised a quarter of the price to the ship captain. In hope that it would be a good start and a different life than what he had experienced in the barren place he was in, the captain agreed on the condition that Mubarak uses use his acquaintances in the village to fill and load the salt, the ship captain did not want to waste any more time.

3rd of Sha'ban 1378 AH (February 10, 1959)

The ship's captain has ordered the anchor to be pulled up and the ready-standing sailors at the bow of the ship have started doing so. They raised their voices with a short sea chant that they divided into two parts that were more fitting for the work and the speed required to pull the thick rope with the anchor at the end of it.

"Whom lived in Tayba, Mohamed With well only mentioned, Mohamed On a Monday was born, Mohamed So was Hassan and Hussain, Mohamed In the valley, he stayed, Mohamed
No food nor water, Mohamed
Faced Al-Kaaba, house of God, Mohamed Prayed 'Oh, Protector,' Mohamed
From hell protect the people of Mohamed."

Wrapped in my blanket, I tried to sleep. The first night after leaving Al Jazer was extremely cold. There were various constellations above my head. "How many of them are there?" I will try to sleep, especially as the ship rocks back and forth due to the waves movement, reminding me of the lullabies my mother sang softly above my bed; Oh, I really miss her.

Her courage and patience when facing the miserable life

and helplessness in our small house located right behind Al Serkal, the big white house with many floors and many rooms. She raised me and my siblings with the wisdom, diligence, and compassion that created rooms in our modest house that are not seen with the eye, but with the heart. The lullabies brought back memories of the old days with all of its details. My peers and I would head to the creek area where we caught big and small fish. Some of us used to place bottles in the creek and later found them filled with fish. While others were satisfied with throwing their rods and waited for whatever fish bit the hook, the youngest of us would place a clay jar covered with a cloth torn at the top where they could gather one small Hassoun (Sillago) fish then they would sing to it the famous song.

Hassoun Bassoon Edkhul min bab Wa ukhroj min bab
Hassoun bassoon
Enter from this door Leave from the other door.

The creek was our favorite place where we learned to fish. We jumped from the tops of the big rickety decks in the middle of it. Maybe I needed this trip to get away with the sailors to appreciate what I used to see every day until it became mundane.

I only dozed off for two hours when Ali called for the dawn prayer with a melodious voice. He was ever so serious and anxious, respected by the sailors. He spoke with them with friendliness however, when the time called for work, he looked stricter. He often sat next to Farhan as they were, as he informed me, neighbors. I recalled the night where Farhan told me about himself.

"The days were difficult when I, my brothers, and all my peers had to get up before dawn to carry the carpenters' breakfast from the big house owned by the ship's captain to the complex of workshops where the big ships were built. The hearts of the great carpenters were harsh on us as if they were devils who never smiled. They toil from after the dawn prayer until just before sunset. They do not speak much during work, except by signs.

"The sounds of the hammers never subside. A cacophonous and loud voice most of the time, sometimes seeming in harmony, they don't rest until after lunch for one hour; one would think they are dead as they never move.

"My stubborn dream was to own my workshop. How disappointingly beautiful are the forgone wishful thinking. I can feel the weight of these wishes tighten my chest. I go to lie at the bow of the ship where there is no one else. I carry my pillow and my duvet to wrap myself in, throw my weight anywhere hoping that my hopes and disappointments will slip away into my pillow so I can throw it overboard. A wishful soul is strenuous for one to bear. I must live without a purpose as it is more blissful than a goal that ultimately ends before it is realized."

He truly knows what he wants from life; he untangles the weaknesses in his life and finds solutions for them. He is looking for a true opportunity. The ambition of a young man in his twenties and the perceptiveness of a man in his eighties; I cannot hide my admiration for him.

4th of Sha'ban 1378 AH (February 11, 1959)

Holding a one-eyed copper telescope, I watched the ship captain approaching in the afternoon. One would think that he is a pirate from the old times; those hardened individuals you hear of. I had never seen him like that. He is tall, wears a turban of Cashmere wool with a black woolen jacket over his white Suri dishdasha. His beard is thick, black, and tinged with white. His complexion has turned a dark golden color due to the reflection of the bright rays of the sun on it.

He looked in one direction intensely. I could not figure it out what he was looking at with my bare eyes. He then ordered the helmsman to turn left toward the east. We moved for half an hour where we saw a big black spot on the horizon and after another hour of sailing, we reached it. We found various boxes of biscuit powder, some of it opened and scattered, forming a large white layer and under them were countless fishes jumping in a strange way while some birds stood on the large boxes and hovered over them.

The boat was lowered to catch the fish by stabbing them with the fishing spears. Minutes later the big boat was filled with medium-sized sharks while the water turned into a large pool of blood around the boat and passed it until it surrounded the ship on all sides.

The skill and speed the sailors displayed while catching the dangerous fish was impressive. The sailors brought some of that powder that seemed to have fallen from one of the passing ships. The boat was raised full of fresh fish while the boxes were left in place. We then took the right heading south.

20th of Sha'ban 1378 AH (February 18, 1959)

We crossed those seas sailing between the Yemeni islands of Socotra and Abd al Kuri. The ship's captain was holding his telescope looking east. A big ship approached us until we were very close. We had finished lunch and some sailors went down to the ships cabin. They lined up in a single line and started taking out the smuggled green boxes. They were heavy in weight; it took two hours to transfer them to the Yemeni ship. Then the ship captain moved with Ali to the other ship, from which they returned minutes later, carrying with them a bag of money, which the ship captain inserted in front of me in his money chest. Then he looked at me and said, "This is the price of the contents of the last weapons store in Muscat, whose owner had died after this trade moved from Muscat to other places. After it stopped during the reign of Sultan Faisal bin Turki, the weapons remained stacked in this store until I bought it for the account of a Yemeni merchant who had come to Muscat a month ago."

We met some ships at the Somali Ras Hafun. Most of them came to Somalia to trade and supply water. Some days I did nothing worth mentioning except teaching the son of the ship's captain and some children the Holy Qur'an, and making them memorize some of the enthusiastic poems of Al-Mutanabbi and Antarah ibn Shaddad. I did not enjoy Farhan's stories anymore; he spoke very little and was absent minded most of the time.

The wind softened before we arrived in Zanzibar. The sailors took advantage to catch large fish, cook them right away and everyone enjoyed eating them. One of the sailors caught a Mahimahi fish and its head was brought to the ship's captain. I was surprised by that because the tribal custom defines that the goat's head goes to the Chief or the Shaikh but not the head of the fish. Then, I was told that it is a marine custom in ships, because the head of this type of fish is very much similar to the Al kamal device used by the ship captain for astronomical measurements in navigation, while the head of the goat is the share of Al-Mjdami (the coxswain) in the sea.

Adjoining the green Pemba Isalnd, was a sign that we reached Zanzibar archipelago and that we are close to our destination, (the island of Angoja) or Zanzibar as Arab sailors call it. Forgetting the long way, we entered a transparent azure sea, behind which appeared the green tall thick coconut palms. The landmarks of the port with many ships scattered in front of the great white government buildings and the houses became clearer. Many ships were scattered in front of the great white government buildings, what a joyful and unforgettable feeling for those who come like us from the land of salt and wasteland!

Zanzibar is the most desirable destinations for sailors, and the most important among African ports. They talked a lot about it on our way and my eagerness to see it exceeded their talk. I imagined that Samha sailed slowly despite the support we got from Al Azyab, the northeast winds. I asked everyone about its details, everyone has a different story there, but they unanimously agreed on its beauty.

Eager for the mainland and the land of Zanzibar, I went down with the first group of the crew after they dropped its anchor. I was overwhelmed by the crowding of the port, and the variety of dresses, faces, and languages. Farhan, the knowledgeable about the country and its affairs, accompanied me this time. I have no doubt that he intends to show off before me about the country he has visited dozens of times before.

The smell of cloves penetrates me, it takes over my whole body, it overwhelms the place, and my sense of smell ignites as it has not done since I was created. I feel great ecstasy mixed with the gentle rain that greeted us from the sea before it. The cold air gives me a refreshing shiver that I have never felt before. I filled my chest with fresh air, and bought us two coconuts to drink its delicious smooth water.

Then we headed to Hadrami Restaurant where we found the crew of the ship called Jamal who had finished their lunch. We shared a table with another sailor from Farhan's friends. A few minutes later, a man with a good manner came to us and took a look at the people sitting, then came to me inquiring.

"You came with the ship Captain Nasser bin Saif?"
"Yeah."
"Thanks to God for your safety." "May God bless you."
"Who is your father?" "Abdullah Al-Moallem."
"May God bless you, my son. Finish your lunch and come drink tea with us," pointing to a table that is not far away.
"If God Wills."
"Ibn Al-Tair, the ship's captain of Jamal ship," said Farhan resentfully, without knowing the reason. He is chatty and does not get tired of talking to anyone. He may turn

aggressive at any moment; be careful of him.

Regardless of Farhan's warning and his chat, I went to where the man was sitting. In his fifties and of medium height possessing the appearance of a ship's captain, with an eagle nose and a full beard. After greeting him, I asked him if he knew the ship Captain Naseer. He replied that they were friends, and that Captain Naseer was born in Sur sixty years ago from a wealthy family with a great maritime heritage. His relationship with the sea at its beginning was not remarkable except that he was spending more hours every day watching through the window of his father's room, which overlooks the sea, where he watched the boys swimming in creek.

He told me when we were young, before his first trip, that his mother had brought him nine Suri dishdashas, sewn with different designs, and she had authorized some of the women who specialized in that to sew them. So he knew for sure that he would sail with his father soon, although she postponed informing him of the matter so that she would forget it herself, as he said.

His father took him when he was not more than thirteen years old. His father was leading one of his ships himself, while the other was in charge of his older brother. As for Jenniat ship, it was driven by another person from outside their family. He is considered one of the most skilled ship captains in Sur and Nasser learned the arts of navigation from him after his father's death.

Seven years later, Nasser entered into a conflict with the elderly of his family, which ended in his favor, after he convinced them that he was the fittest to lead the largest ship. Despite the fact that he was only twenty that year, he offered them the big house that he inherited from his father as a mortgage as a guarantee to take in case the ship is exposed to any navigational risks.

Nasser bin Saif led his first ship, the Jenniat, and its name attributed to the golden pounds as one of the workers found a bag filled with gold in the place that was prepared to install the ship's main shaft and its base, which is called locally (Al-Hiraab), and it was built from that money after the worker was well-rewarded.

He was a good omen for his family a good-luck charm for them. He is a well-educated ship captain, there is no doubt about that, but Sur is full of other well-educated. He succeeded in what he pledged to them, which enabled him to manage the seven ships of the family in addition to his command of the largest of them.

His most notable success was in his suggestion that they allocate one of their ships to one destination throughout the year, during which they only import rice. This idea made a big difference in raising the income of his family, especially during the days of the Great Depression and the hunger that afflicted the region, where the demand for rice was great. His mother was the happiest person with his achievements and she pledged to him to search for the best girl in Sur to marry, and it was.

Ibn Al Tair stopped talking, then he remained silent for a long time, so that I could not find anything to say after his long talk about the ship's captain. I asked him for permission to leave, and he nodded 'yes' without uttering the word.

How does a man know all the details about another? I listened to the captain of the ship, Jamal, marveling at his knowledge of the Captain;s biography, and narrating long talk about Captain Nasser, as if he was waiting to be asked about

Captain Naseer.These are details that only a brother, a close friend, or a bitter rival knows. I more wondered about ending his speech in a strange way? He mentioned the issue of the captain's marriage with bitterness; a woman must have entered between them. I asked Farhan, who immediately answered me affirmatively, saying, "It is a well-known news; she was the cousin of Ibn al-Tair."

25th of Sha'ban 1378 AH
(March 4, 1959)

Five days were the most incredible days of my life during which I entered the cinema for the first time. I watched a movie called Samson about the story of a mighty man destroying himself and his enemies; I ate different meals; I saw Omani castles and many monuments; I attended the Friday prayer in a mosque as half of the prayer was in Arabic, and I took part slightly in teaching sessions.

We then set out to sail to the Rufiji Delta to load a large shipment of al-Jandal wood (mangrove timber), which we would use back home for roofing.

Our trip was a terrible experience. A gloomy and suffocating atmosphere of heat and humidity with heavy, endless rain. After which we returned complaining of illnesses and diseases that we had not known before.

It was a journey of weakness. Long days of endless torment with swarms of ferocious mosquitoes that shredded our bodies, like an army that dominates people, spreading disease everywhere.

A mythical paradise in appearance with magnificent tall trees, coiled plants, and drenched underbrush. It is not compared to what the eyes see of bliss with what the bodies suffer from a deadly poisonous world. Hippos galloping and big stalking crocodiles; the different sounds of animals, uninterrupted cries, wondrous shapes of colorful birds, armies of insects, and small snakes are raining down on us from the top of the trees.

This is the Rufiji River Delta (Simba Ranga). The most loathsome voyage for both me and the crew and there is no turning back. The biggest goal of the voyage to East Africa is the mangrove timber that grows in that bleak part of the world and is in great demand in the northern Gulf, where it sold for a good price. Samha was moving in a leisurely manner within a serpentine lane. All the way, the ship's captain had a sharp sight and the sailors were silent. Their previous experience of the place explained to me the reason for the gloomy atmosphere that I understood too late.

The boats of the strong black local workers approached us and blocked our way. Initially, I thought they were pirates. Samha's engines were stopped and they came up to us like fighters armed with rusty saws and axes. Covered only by simple tattered garments, red eyes, and large swollen lips, their black bodies stained with blotchy, fearsome looks, they had a good look in their faces that sends reassurance to those who watch them. They circled us asking for food, which was soon brought to them. With insatiable hunger they eat, and then lay asleep on the roof of Samha which continued its way along that infernal sea lane.

Samha let down her anchor where fate has ordained a piece of mud and sand that formed an island on the riverbank. We thought it was our haven to move over instead of the boring deck, had it not been for a huge crocodile taking over it made us change our minds. Not far from us was a dense forest of mangroves, which is the site of the loggers. The workers slowly got down heading into the midst of the thick trees. Armed with saws and a few axes that work just enough to cut down the very tough trees we need.

For half a day, their only food was dates and sufficient water to live on. Their weapon against mosquitoes was a circular flyswatter, with which they hit their bodies with full force, killing hundreds of the mosquito army that gathered around them every time and the blood sucked from their bodies became black masses on their skins.

My way to keep mosquitoes away from me was to use some clove oil and thyme, which I had bought from Zanzibar to take with me as a gift for my mother. I apply it to my whole body twice a day. It helped me very much, despite the number of bites I got. I told Ali, Farhan and some sailors of this recipe, but they preferred to be patient with the affliction or to use mosquito nets, which did not work, as they became like fishing nets that had become outdated for the fishermen after it had worn out.

The miserable group of Africans arrived before sunset, their lips sore and their eyes getting redder, bringing the mangrove poles loaded onto the boats. They climbed aboard with their scratched, bleeding bodies. They throw their weak bodies for an hour on the surface after which they treat themselves with whatever traditional medicines are available to them on the ship. They then ate what they had of their food and slept without grumbling. How hard life is when people are not given many choices to choose from!

You do not hear from them the slightest sound. Their bodies were spoilt by stings, but they do not grumble but rather live in the hope that another ship will carry them in order to fetch money, a fate heavier than Samha. But to me, it was lighter for them than the rain showers that greeted us when we arrived. It is a life that we did not choose, but it chose us, as the voyage that was repeated in my dreams chose me. Every night, an old man would dress me in a garment made of a sail. Yes, from the sails of ships, so I become heavier than Samha and went down to a dark place until my pulse stopped, then I floated again.

Our sailors faced some different injuries as well. Due to the nature of the wooden ship which is full of sharp-edged wood that may inflict severe injuries during the night or while loading, or perhaps injuries due to slipping on the wet surface sometimes. They were treated by traditional methods used by sailors, in which thick salt is mixed with hot water as a base for it until they reach a port where the injured are taken for treatment in a hospital.

I spent in that place half of the month of Ramadan. I did not have days like the days I spent in this place. Neither fasting nor prayers were as they should be, and if it is not for patience and modesty, I would have left Samha and its people and left with the first ship leaving for Zanzibar. I was praying with all my heart that time passes quickly and end what we came for.

After twenty days, the health of the workers and crew weaken. It was an infected environment full of disease, mold, and fatigue, and would have killed some of us without God's mercy. I was tired of waiting in that place after experiencing the pleasant atmosphere of Zanzibar. I am running out of patience but Ali is telling me that we will leave in two days when the shipment of timber will be complete. I was relieved to hear that, and I felt wellness running through my body after being emaciated.

19th of Shawwal 1378 AH (April 27, 1959)

The time to go back came nearer; the Kos winds (the northeast wind that comes from the sea) have started to blow and some of the ships have left. We were concerned for Mubarak, the salt seller, as he has made a profit of his trade but the new environment he witnessed here has tempted him, he only scarcely returned to the ship. We heard that he planned to marry a woman of an Arab decedent whom he found working in a farm and was infatuated with her. He was thinking of settling down in Zanzibar to escape his harsh life.

I was preparing myself to head toward the Grand Mosque in Zanzibar where I saw students studying books on Sufism with their scholar Sheikh Abdul Qadir Al-Haddad, next thing I know I heard Farhan calling me.

"Did you hear the news, Aqeel?" "Good ones I hope."

"Obaid arrived on one of the Suri ships a week ago in Zanzibar, brought his savings, and bought large quantities of ghee and cloves, to be shipped and traded in Oman."

"It is within his right to do that; he is a free man."

"That is not the issue; he is planning to ship his goods on Samha."

"What is wrong with that?"

"You are naïve, son!" Farhan laughed loudly repeating, "Ibn Salma did it again."

"What was the ship captain's response?"

"He said nothing; he is a merchant above all. Obaid will pay for his cargo anyway. Although I saw Ali fuming with rage."

"Where is he now?" "Right with the sailors."

I headed to where Obaid was supervising the fastening of his goods on the deck; he stood ever so clam and elegant. I extended my hand to congratulate him on starting his trade, gone was the recklessness he displayed at the beginning of the trip; he asked me to sit down.

"You must be curious about the reason I escaped, are you not, Aqeel?"

"Indeed, I would like to know that."

"I will tell you everything. I was born in Sur to a woman brought from the middle of the Arabian Peninsula in a year so grim that is called the Year of Hunger. A year in which a severe famine occurred; where some people were forced to sell their children for fear that they would perish. When she was eleven years old, her father brought her and her sister, who was one year older, to the outskirts of Oman. He handed them to a merchant he knew in Adam Market so they can work in his house for a while, the merchant then moved to Sur with his family when his trade was booming there, he rented a house then bought it.

"My uncle arrived in Sur, nine years after the displacement of my mother and sister from Najd. My grandfather had sent him to search for them and take them back with the promise of a financial reward for whoever finds them with him, and upon his arrival to the house of the merchant, he was hosted and welcomed. He met his two sisters, the eldest of which had married several months ago, and they preferred to stay with their husbands, especially since they learned of the death of their mother and that their father was old and his memory began to fade while he lived with his son, my aunt was pregnant at that time. My mother married my father, who worked for the father of the ship captain, although he is fifteen years older than her, he was in good health and loved by the family. I loved my mother very much for her kindness that embraces everyone, which harmed her greatly, she sacrificed all her time at the expense of her health, for the service of the lady of the big house, and for the satisfaction of my father, who had commanded her to do that. Her affection toward me infuriated my father who never stopped complaining that she will spoil me and I will never be able to persevere to the challenges which people like us face.

"My father was respected by the ship captain even though he is only five years older than him, this was attributed to an incident the captain always told us of in which my father saved the ship captain from drowning when they were just boys learning how to swim with their peers on the shore of the big creek. I never got tired of the story and I used to brag about it to my peers.

"When I was ten, the ship captain suggested to my father that I would work as a 'Walid Sherbeh' (water boy) in their travels that season; it is a job where a child hand out water to sailors while they work encouraging them to continue working. He immediately agreed to pull me away from my mother and her spoiling of me, as he put it. Also, to teach me carpentry which he mastered in the long spare time on the deck after becoming a capable sailor. That was nine years ago. "They took care of us greatly; I cannot deny that. They gave my father and mother a house, although it was small but was comfortable and most of our supplies came from the big house. The ship captain, although strict at times, he and his wife were incredibly generous toward us, however, I always loathed our status as slaves.

"Why did my father have to run pouring the coffee for the men? It always happens, every time! I hated that scene; it made me forget everything good they did, they had broken something in him that can never be repaired. I hated them and their ignorant, arrogant children that sat at the head of every seating without any merits but their white skin and their parents' wealth.

"I did not know where to go to escape this miserable state? Should I bequeath it upon my children as well? I postponed my marriage until God change this situation, I could not immigrate and leave my father and my mother, whom I adored, behind. Only the money would change many things but how would I get my hands on it when I am a mere sailor with no hope to change that? I then realized that freedom was my salvation. I pre-empted it and took it the way you saw, and I don't regret it. It is not fair that it continues like this forever, don't you agree, Aqeel? Surely my condition will change from now on, it will definitely change!"

Before Obaid could finish what he was saying, a sailor approached us telling Obaid to go meet the ship Captain Nasser. I looked at Obaid who appeared clearly flustered unsure what to do; it reminded me of the faces of the children that run away from their teachers at the school in Sur. It was the first time Obaid will stand face to face in front of Captain Nasser after he fled in Muscat; I wonder how will it go?
"I will be right there," he informed the sailor.

I suggested that he take Farhan with him to support him

and he quickly replied, "I will ask him that." He was like a drowning man being thrown a lifeline, he walked away looking for Farhan. I did not want to miss this event so I went first to the captain using his son's assignment to memorize Surat Al-Mujadila and recite it tomorrow as an excuse.

Moments later, Obaid and Farhan walked up, followed by Ali who stood next to the captain. I pretended to be busy talking to his son. Obaid's eyes fell on me and I got embarrassed, but then Captain Nasser initiated the talk before Obaid.

"Praise be to God that you arrived safely, Obaid."

"Thank you, Uncle Nasser, how are you?" "Good, thanks to God."

"Glad for that."

"I hope you bought the goods successfully."

"Yes, indeed. I am extremely thankful that you agreed to load it."

"Son, we are merchants, and this is our job, whoever pays for the shipment, we deliver it for him."

"I will pay what you ask if God wills, Uncle Nasser." "We will discount off the cost, Obaid. You are one of us and you deserve it more than any other."

"I would not expect any less of you, Uncle Nasser." "Tell me, Obaid, why did you sail with us from Sur if you had previously intended to get your freedom in such a manner? We lost a valuable crewmember that we depended on. If we knew before that we would have brought a replacement."

Ali intruded unable to stop himself. "Samha is now sailing with one less crewmember." The captain turned to him, commanding him to remain silent.

"It just happened," Obaid answered tight-lipped.

"Was it not more appropriate to apologize to us at least before you ask that your cargo would be shipped in Samha, which you had deliberately chosen from several Suri ships in the port?"

Shame was now prominent on Obaid's face as rage became more apparent in the captain's expression. Only then, Farhan interfered to defend Obaid.

"The situation of Obaid and his family should have ended a long time ago, captain. There are only three families in Sur in this state."

"Were we ever negligible toward him and his family? You know more than anyone how well we treated his mother Farhan. We married her to Sebit, the best worker we had, and we also provided them with a house behind ours. Obaid was raised with the big house children with nothing left to be desired. Is that how he pays us back?"

"Slavery is harsh and one cannot compare any gifts to being deprived of freedom. We live in a different time now; look at Zanzibar now. It developed even more than the motherland of Oman in many things. The people here are running their country well after they were liberated."

"Do you prefer if you lived here still, Farhan? Things are regarded according to the time. At that time, poverty and war were the usual. Prisoners were murdered and children were not spared. The white traders recommended that they sell them and benefit from them. I also have documents that prove that the Arabs were not the most prominent slavers. Most of them were Africans and some were Europeans widely spread in Africa."

"No one knows what would have happened, and we do not know how it would have turned out to be if we stayed here. What I am certain of is that my family who were chained up and taken from these areas was not happy to leave."

"It was not us who have taken them Farhan. 'No soul burdened with sin will bear the burden of another.' We were all born in Sur, and this how it was. You also know that Obaid's mother was brought here from the center of the Arabian Peninsula due to the famine. Her family was the one seeking to save her from starving to death by selling her in Oman."

"Have you also forgotten how some of the old ship captains, when they filled their ships cargo hold with sugar and before leaving East Africa, they asked the poor black children to take what they wanted from it so that if a large number of them gathered in the heart of the ship they closed the gate of the cargo hold and then fled to sell them in Oman?" "How many of them did that? Two? Three? Hundreds of ships coming from Sur to replenish the economy of the country and benefited its people. You know very well that the slaves in Sur were officially liberated by an initiative of the people there before all the other regions and they owned their own homes and they were treasured by many wealthy people."

I was listening to that heated debate between Farhan and the ship captain, which I was responsible for by my suggestion to Obaid that Farhan accompany him when confronting the captain. I did not realize that the slave buried within the depth of Farhan would move to become a giant heavier than Samha. A giant who knows how the years of oppression a person faces can impose a fate upon them turning them into a second-class human. A class that is only determined by how humane is their master. Often, fabricated humanity does not believe that all people were equal. That makes the so-called slaves board a boat of indignity so they can buy their dignity back by placing what's left of their dignity under the Al-Balooz flag (The British Embassy).

Unexpectedly, Captain Nasser finished the discussion quietly, "Anyway, it is all good, Obaid. You have done well buying cloves and ghee. They have a popular market in Oman, just as you did well to bring Farhan to defend you."

I walked away followed by Obaid and Farhan whom I expected would be happy about his argument with the captain, however, he looked at Obaid with rage and said, "This is the first time that I have argued with Captain Nasser and it is all because of you Obaid. It is certainly your fault. You intended to escape after you have signed a contract to travel with us. You have chosen Samha to load your cargo of all Suri ships left to satisfy something in your sick mind. Maybe to brag to your fellow sailors or perhaps to challenge the captain himself. Have you forgotten the compassion that the captain and his family showed you? The worst of all how you did not go to greet the captain upon boarding the ship. You only asked Ali to ask for his permission that you load the cargo. These are not your father's manners, nor your mother's character. You put me in an awkward position with the good man who did not chase you out but gave you a discount!"

Words seemed to have fled Obaid. He weakly suggested that he go back to Captain Nasser to kiss his head in apologies. However, Farhan refused after the matter had reached such a heated argument between them.

I was astonished by Farahan more than his previous controversy with the captain. How did he defend Obaid bitterly if he believed that Obaid was wrong? And why did he blame him now if he thought he was mistaken? Is it to back a brother whether he is wrong or not? How did he stand up against the captain so strongly? I wonder how did he yield such authority to argue?

20th of Shawwal 1378 AH (April 28, 1959)

One day is left to go back to Oman, I've missed the neighborhoods of Sur very much, especially my favorite hobby of walking between the narrow alleys before sunset where these roads are filled with the wonderful fragrance of frankincense. There the camel caravans, loaded with dates, Omani lemons and various goods, crisscross that long alley called Sikat Alboush (the alley of the Camels).

For two centuries, Sur dominated the sea business in Oman. It is no longer the same since the circumstances changed after the discovery of oil. The sons of the ship captains and those who depended on them to complete their fathers' journey are leaving the city. The Gulf countries now have attractive opportunities for work and study. Most of the ships have stopped their journeys and some of them have been sold. The luxury that the ships brought resulted in an idle generation that avoid the risk of working in the sea like their fathers. Their motto is the saying, "Why exhaust yourself fighting the waves when you can lay on the shore."

God help these sailors who spend eight months every year on the deck of these ships living on memories. There is no doubt that their feelings are overwhelming in their first week of travel but as they continue sailing, they tend to forget. Then all these feelings appear with a great intensity shortly before they return home.

Most of the ships left the port of Zanzibar, racing back home though a few ships remain. The chances of Samha reaching home before the rest of the ships are great because the captain takes a direct way back, as I heard, passing through only one coastal city to supply water. Everyone is excited to see their families soon. The sailors will throw a party tonight and Captain Nasser has ordered a dinner for the crews of the Gulf and Omani ships remaining in the port.

The sailors of Sur bring life to the dead places with their songs, chants and drums that never remain silent. They drum when the anchor and sails are raised, when they are lowered, and when they arrive and leave. It even gets louder during boat races. It seems to me that they drum even for the funerals and only become silent when the wind stops and the ship stands still, the matter they hate the most, but with the engines now in place, there is no need for their silence.

A large number of sailors gathered on the quay that night. They sat and shared various tales while the captain ordered that a luxurious Persian carpet be laid with a few cushions put around it. Sweets and coffee were served to them before their main meal of rice and fresh meat.

Samha's crew bid farewell to their guests with drums and marine dances in which other crews participated. I saw Farhan dancing as if he was thirty years old. The guests thanked Captain Nasser for his hospitality. While our sailors completed their celebration on the quay, the cook was busy preparing coal for the hookah for the captain and the coxswain.

I was amazed at the strength of the Samha crew's affiliation to it, and I did not know at first whether this was due to the character of the captain or the nature of people defending their source of living. The strange thing is that, despite all the differences between the crew, their enthusiasm for their ship and their defense of crew was very noticeable to me.

It is the character of the captain, no doubt. They follow him without hesitation like they are bewitched. I was told that one time the cargo of a Suri ship in Kismayo, Somalia, was attacked by some locals, which coincided with the passage of the ship captain with some of his sailors, so he ordered the thieves to return the cargo, but they refused and started insulting him; so the sailors attacked the thieves very quickly in defense of the captain in a battle of hands and sticks that did not take long before the thieves fled. The ship's captain turned the event into a celebration, gathering dozens of men from the various ships crews in the place. The sailors confirm that he supports them with money, and personally attends their occasions such as marriages and funerals and others.

The amount of rice with meat that I devoured that night was the reason that I went to sleep right after, and not a moment passed until I felt a lot of movement and screaming. I was terrified and saw the cook fighting a big fire that was burning on the roof as some sailors helped him in trying to put it out. Soon the pace of the fire increased until it destroyed a large part of the front deck of Samha. I approached the mast, and had it not been for the determination of our sailors and the help of the sailors of the neighboring ships who rushed to help, the fire would have consumed the entirety of Samha. Most of the goods stacked on the quay, fortunately, have not been lifted to the ship.

I quickly descended from the ship's staircase with some passengers who came two days before sailing. The sailors managed to put out the fire after great exertion. It seemed clear that Samha would be late in leaving more than it already was until the deck was completely repaired and returned as it was. I saw the captain talking to Ali in anger, moving his hands nervously and pointing them in different directions, though I did not hear what he was saying. I saw Farhan checking the place of the damage. He seemed to be distracted by what had happened. I approached him but he did not notice me; he seemed confused. I excused him being that most of the work will be on him, which will take more than a month I think.

Captain Nasser and the coxswain came while I was with Farhan, I did not say anything. The captain asked Farhan, "How do you assess the situation?"

He answered, "A month, I need a whole month."

The captain interrupted him, saying, "We cannot wait a whole month, we will lose the wind of return. You have ten days; we will work day and night and everyone will be at your service."

Farhan protested against the suggested time. The destruction is great on the deck and it needs complete reconstruction. In addition, nothing pleases Captain Nasser but perfection. He is the only carpenter in the ship and the rest will bring him only what he needs, and the real work will fall on his shoulders. The captain ordered then to search for local carpenters to help Farhan to finish work in ten days.

The carpenters and the ship's crew continued to work day and night while some travelers left for other ships for fear of delay. The work was completed within the specified time for Farhan. He showed a tremendous energy that exceeded his age, during which he did not speak much as usual, but he became addicted to insults to African workers and he urged them to continue working. I heard him speaking to them in Swahili and saying:

Indelini Covania Kazy

This old man always surprises me.

Ali asked me, "What do you think about Samha's deck now?"

"More beautiful than ever."

I suggested rewarding Farhan for his great effort. Ali assured that the captain would keep him on the ship after his work.

What does it mean 'keep him on the ship?' Is there an intention to send him out? A slip of the tongue from Ali that he did not notice, and I understood from it that the captain did not like it when Farhan supported Obaid publicly, and decided to give up his services next season.

Captain Nasser was happy to complete the work even though we were nine days late due to the negligence of the cook, who was fired on the same day. The captain does not accept those who are not good at their work, and it seems that he refuses to be challenged as well. The cook is not from the main crew of the ship anyway. He left today on a ship to Muscat where he belongs. Ali assigned the sailor Fayz to his work, as he is a skilled cook as well, who accepted this temporary job.

While I was talking to Ali we saw the captain, dressed as usual, heading to Barzat of Yemeni auctioneers. Sitting with the rest of the ship captains was their chief Ben Jarnah and his friend Baharun. All the captains of Sur trade with these two merchants. I asked Ali about his relationship with Captain Nasser and the secret of his joy, activeness, and happiness, despite the tragedy of the fire that postponed our trip.

That is his happy nature that we have known since his childhood and it did not change until that day when the pilgrims from Gwadar arrived at Sur carrying with them the Smallpox that later killed hundreds of the people of the city.

The disease spread rapidly in the small town, causing great panic among the people, and the atmosphere became bleak. There were no hospitals or medicines for it except for traditional medicines, which were successful if the disease was superficial. As those who got sores in their mouths were considered dead, unless God blessed them with his mercy.

The death was flying above our heads in the city. Funerals were coming from everywhere on a daily basis for two months; most of them children and the elderly. This caused us a lot of sadness, although people did not know the reason at first due to the shock and quick spread of the epidemic until the news seemed to be spreading that the pilgrims were the ones who came carrying death in their clothes to us.

His caring mother died due to the illness, which constituted a major turning point in changing his personality, and sadness became his companion. He was different when he was with his mother. His strong personality changed and he becomes meek in her presence. He used to deliberately exaggerate the righteousness of her on all occasions. She made sure that conditions were created for him to continue living in prosperity after the death of his father, especially after his uncles carved out a large part of his farm during the period of their guardianship over him. She did not care about that and sold her property to support her son. She succeeded in that until he grew up a strong and reliable man.

The captain's wife was seven months pregnant when his

mother died. He decided to name his son after his grandfather from his mother's side in her honor, and to allow his wife to choose the name if the baby was a girl. So one day, and while he was enjoying his time with the other captains one morning and the talk of illness seized every conversation, someone came telling him that they need him immediately in his house. He found himself in front of his beloved wife, who was bedridden, and the fever had taken a major toll on her, and she was suffering from severe pain and headache accompanied by nausea. He expected it to be a passing fever, but her sister setting next to her mentioned that it could be the symptoms of smallpox. The captain was shocked and ordered to prepare her to take her to his farm with her sister to isolate her and treat her there with traditional medicines, hoping to save her life and the life of the son he has been waiting for.

His wife's illness affected him a lot. She was the compassionate heart and the only refuge for him after his mother, who left him a month ago. After that, he met with the elite of the people, and took a very tough decision to exile the remaining sick pilgrims to an isolated area and leave them there to face their fate with some provisions to rid the city of the cause of the spreading epidemic.

Someone suggested reopening the houses of Al-Mujdar, which are stone houses for sanitary isolation on top of a hill near the city. They were used in the past to isolate those who had infectious diseases. Then he ordered people not to mix with each other except for the utmost necessity, and then he with some young people burned the pilgrims' camp after it was emptied of its residents.

His wife managed to survive after suffering, and gave birth to his young son who accompanies us on this journey.

He was born very weak due to his mother's illness, but he recovered quickly and did not leave his father after he reached the age of nine. His father insisted on bringing him with us to get used to the sea and its horrors early. I pity the poor child. He should have been with his peers playing in the lanes of Sur there, or he should have studied at your uncle's school, Aqeel, instead of going through the sea and its horrors.

That incident keeps coming back to the captain's mind and he feels guilty for what happened. Despite the epidemic causing the death of his mother and the illness of his wife, you can see an apparent sadness in his eyes that does not subside, except when he is preoccupied with what he loves; such times are like when Samha is in a race with another ship. Then his sadness turns into a flame of determination that he pours on those working with him. One shout from him is capable of inflaming their enthusiasm. Then, once the victory ceremony ends, the sadness returns to his eyes, after the victory ceremony to which he is accustomed.

For nine years, he feels that he is to blame for the death of the leader of the pilgrims and those with him. Until that day, five days after the fire broke out in Samha, I was with the ship captain and some Hadhrami merchants in an Indian exchange shop when a non-Arab man who spoke Arabic entered the shop and greeted us. He asked Captain Nasser, do you remember me? He looked at him in astonishment and after a period of silence, the captain asked, "Are you the head of the pilgrims from Gwadar?"

"In the flesh."

"How can I not remember you as your face did not leave me one night? I thought you were dead, what happened to you and what brought you here?"

"I left the profession of taking pilgrims to the holy lands after that unfortunate incident of the epidemic, and worked for years in my father-in-law's farm. I then decided to buy a boat from one of the Kuwaiti merchants. I have been told that they sell their wooden boats cheap after discovering oil. I decided to travel on it as a money owner because I have no knowledge of navigation."

"Did you manage to buy a boat here?"

"Looks like I'm late. I'm going to Kuwait. I was told there are a lot of ships for sale there."

"God brought you to me to see you. The Kuwaitis do not sell their ships here. You will go with us. By God's will you will be in my hospitality until we reach Sur where you can buy a boat from there as well, or I will arrange a boat for you to Kuwait, but will you tell me your name?"

"Jawad."

"Thanks to God you are safe, Jawad."

"What you offer me is a lot, this is very generous of you." "I'm glad; tell me, did anyone die in that tent with you?" "A young man, under eighteen, had been debilitated by epidemic before he was transferred from Sur."

Then Captain Nasser hugged Jawad and congratulated him on his safety again. Then we all went to one of the religious men the captain knew, and he asked him about the manslaughter blood money. The religious man told the captain to pay several thousands of shillings, which he immediately gave to Jawad and begged him to deliver them to the young boy's family. Jawad was in great astonishment because the captain didn't have to do this, the disease was the killer, not him, but he took the money promising to deliver it to the boy's family.

I then saw a cloud of sadness leave the face of Captain Nasser forever, and joy replaced it. Nasser, whom we had known for a long time, came back to us. He muttered words from which I only heard the repetition of the letter H, while he pulled a pipe from his pocket to take a different breath this time. He turned to me after that and said, "Even the fires have life, Ali. If the surface of Samha had not been burned and we were late, we would not have met Jawad."

1st of Dhu'l-Qi'dah 1378 AH (May 8, 1959)

We will leave Zanzibar after two hours. This luxurious port was managed in an advanced way in which dozens of characters of different origins take part in the work. During the three months we waited for the return wind called Al-Kos, we sailed in the delta of the Rufiji River to bring timber. I went to where the ship's captain stood and he asked me about my opinion of Zanzibar. I told him that it was a great port, run in an orderly manner by the Omani rulers, and that it was more flourishing than Oman. I expected that it would not last as the Indian merchants controlled the market and I caught a flare-up in the eyes of the local workers that might change the condition. The Omanis are not aware of that, as they are busy enjoying their lives.

Samha was filled with travelers. The number of women was so big that I wondered how they would all fit into that room and how they would be with children who need care and space. It is the hardship of life, and the search for a decent life, that forces people to take risks and search for a better life.

The ship's captain had asked the coxswain and some sailors to go to bring Mubarak to the ship gently, and if he refused, he must be brought by force, saying, "It seems that the Zanzibari clove made him forget the salt of his land, and that whoever gets used to the cold Zanzibar air can no longer bear the heat of the Omani desert."

A great desire burned within me to see my home, a desire that was untouched by the beauty of the forests and palaces of Zanzibar. I pledged myself that when I go back to Sur I will enjoy watching the shipbuilding workshops; following the movement of people; listening to the sounds of shipbuilding hammers; talking to the elderly and visiting the carpenters and the ship captains; enjoying with them seeing the ships rise off the ground piece by piece; now that I have experienced the sea and the life therein.

I was with the captain listening to his son reciting a poem from Imam Al-Shafi'i's poetry to us, when the coxswain came to tell him that the crew of the ship Jamal are challenging Samha in the race from Zanzibar to Ras Hafun, which is a long distance to race. What do they intend?

"Ibn Altair again? Is it not enough for them that we have defeated them last season?"

"He wants to avenge his previous defeat in Basra."

"I'm afraid the engine will let us down. I don't know what happened to it despite all the maintenance we did for it in India. I will buy a new engine for Samha after this season."

"Tell them to go ahead before us by half a day and Samha is able to defeat them after that."

"It would be considered an insult."

In the afternoon, Jamal's crew were beating their drums and singing very excitedly. What are they planning for? What are their intentions?

The ship (Jamal) hit its bells, their drums beat increased, his sailors danced, they pointed to us in a shameful sign that indicated a real challenge in the race. The ship captain went mad in a way I was not familiar with him before. We haven't started yet, what happened to him?

He declared, threateningly, that he would burn Samha and her crew alive if we lost the race. Is he joking? Do sailors have much to do than direct the sails where he commands them? Undoubtedly, Jamal's inappropriate festivity angered him.

The anchor was lifted, ready to set sail. The singer sang loudly again:

The singer: yo-ho-ho, God is the Most Generous Sailors: He is God
The singer: Oh, the All-Mighty, The Most Merciful Sailors: He is God
The singer: traveling in the protection of God Sailors: If God Wills

The singer: Praying for good wind and easy voyage and help from God, Al Fatiha to the Prophet. We all recited Al Fatiha, and we trusted in God. The great sail was quickly raised then the sailors stood in a circle singing enthusiastically. The beating of their rough feet reached the crew of the ship Jamal.

Oh Muscat, come closer to me,
There is no deity but God, we praise Him.
Looking for the day, I will see the beautiful girls of Sur,
There is no deity but God, we praise Him.

The eyes of the sailor responsible of the rudder were on the road, and Ali was provoked by the enthusiastic singing and applauded from his place, but the eyes of the ship's captain did not deviate from Jamal's ship. Mubarak had arrived at Samha an hour ago waiting to talk to the captain.

As Ali told him, he did not know that it was the day of sailing, because he was absent out the ship for days unlike what other people do. He tried to get off the ship after it lifted its anchor, but it had moved, so he came complaining to the ship's captain, who told him to jump into the sea if he wanted to return to his fiancée, Mubarak became calm and accepted the reality. Then, he told the ship captain that he did not propose to anyone, but only spoke to her father about the matter.

Leaning on one side of Samha, who was sailing challenging, I saw Jawad sitting near Mubarak who seemed to be wandering and had not spoken to anyone since we left Zanzibar. The sailors were all the way joking about his love story for the girl he left behind and they blamed him for not jumping out of the ship for her, and he did not answer.

To escape from boredom, I approached Jawad to ask him what happened to him during the days of the disease in Sur and how he survived. I found him sitting silently looking at the horizon. He was a good-natured man, with a huge body, white with visible redness, age about forty and he spoke Arabic well. I told him that I was twelve at the time, and that I had heard that they were dark days, so that they were dated and it was called the year of smallpox.

"After the disease spread in my body, they decided to banish me outside Sur, like the rest of the pilgrims. A group of rebellious young men caught me. The ship's captain was the leader of the group. They tied my hand with such a force that the rope sank in my flesh and they put me on a donkey they had with them. I twisted with pain but my unbridled nature and my pride would not allow me to make a sound of anguish in front of anyone because of my terrible suffering.

"They carried me on a fierce day on obstinate donkey, I

was exhausted because it kept stopping and my body was piled on the saddle like a large piece of fat that vibrates with every movement. I thought that I would transmit the disease to the poor donkey because of me clinging so hard to it. I felt dizzy due to the dryness of my body because of this exhausting path. I asked myself, 'will I ever see my beloved daughter and her mother again?' After that I passed out for a long time, after which the men and the rope that tied me disappeared. I woke up and saw a yellow color covering my entire body, and three golden human statues in front of me. I thought it was a dream until a Bedouin appeared to me and told me that he found me lying unconscious near the tent in which he found the three pilgrims whom I thought were statues of gold at first. He took care of us by the only method he knew, which is to smear our bodies with yellow turmeric mixed with water after heating it. Afterwards, he pierced the abscesses swollen with pus with the tip of his dagger and cleaned them. He informed me that the disease had spread among them for a long time, and he saw his father treating his brothers that way.

"Unfortunately, he could not save the boy Murad for his condition was very bad. When he found him, the abscesses had spread in his body and inside his mouth. He tried to prolong his stay with his camel's milk after heating it, but to no avail. He guided me to his grave to read Al-Fatihah for him. My friends were getting better, and he assured that my treatment would not take a long time.

"After that I learned from the Bedouin who goes to Sur once a week, that the healthy pilgrims, and those who recovered from them, were transferred by a ship to the holy lands and that the epidemic is about to end there after the people of Sur lost dozens of children, elderly, some young men and four of the pilgrims, whom I didn't know. Then we decided to go to the port of Muscat with one of the caravans to complete the way to the pilgrimage from there after the noble Bedouin provided us with a date and some silver coins. When we arrived Muscat, we decided to return to Gwadar. We hired an Iranian wooden boat to pay him when we arrived there, because the health of those with me, despite the end of the symptoms of the disease, did not allow them to continue the path to Hajj, and the Hajj season was about to end.

"After several days, we arrived at Gwadar to the surprise of the people. The news had reached them mistakenly, by some sailors, that most of the pilgrims had died of this disease so there was mourning and a state of sadness prevailed in all of Gwadar. Then, when they saw us, at first they thought that we were the ones left from that campaign, but I hastened to reassure them that most of the pilgrims are fine, and they have completed their journey to the holy lands, and that the number of the dead is only five, and this was like the return of the soul to our entire region."

2nd of Dhu'l-Qi'dah 1378 AH (May 9, 1959)

It never crossed my mind that Farhan's luck would finally smile at him as the land of Al Jazer received Samha's anchor generously and his wishes that he dreamed of since I knew him would be fulfilled in moments. He talked to me about that on the second day of the race just after I had my breakfast. Unlike his nature, I saw him leaving the window he was working on and leaning on the side of the ship. I went to him and he looked me straight in the eye. Another person appeared to me; two laughing eyes, a jovial face, a slight tremor in his hand, and as his left eye was twitching quickly, he seemed suspicious.

I was curious about what I saw. Did something happen to him or did his obsession increase this time until it controlled his nerves and left him as I saw? He seemed different from what I left him a few hours ago; he is not the one I was with yesterday. He indicated to me to approach him and without introductions he told me what happened with him.

"The night that we first cast our anchors in Al-Jazer on our way to Zanzibar, I tried to fall asleep a little. I lay in the bow of the ship, alone, near the anchor so as not to hear the noise of the sailors. As soon as I tried to sleep, I was disturbed by the cacophony of sounds that kept knocking on the side of the ship from the front and just below me where I had chosen that place.

The sound was coming and going! I asked myself, "Is it a dead fish with which the wave moves throwing it on the ship and bringing it back again?" I hated that continuous knocking and I cursed it repeatedly, whatever's there. Then I gave up after saying that it is undoubtedly a call to me. Everything around us speaks to us in its own language in this life, whether someone understands it or not. This is what I heard from the preacher of the mosque one day. As I moved myself a little to the side of the ship and turned my head outside to look down, a pungent aroma penetrated me. A sticky gray mass like cow dung. I hadn't quite figured it out yet and then the smell reminded me of itself again. I was struck, frozen until I almost fell. Is it what I think it is? I asked myself without stopping, "Has God answered my supplications with such speed and generosity? Did this piece hold together to knock on wood to make my dream come true?" I held it, smelled it, realized its color, hugged it, and kissed it. A large piece of ambergris, sailor's dream, finally became in my possession and at that speed. "O Aqeel, do you believe it is a sign of imminent good that will happen inevitably?"

I asked him eagerly, "Do you mean the perfume of ambergris, Farhan?"

"The floating jewel of the sea, the expensive perfume O Aqeel, yes. Sperm whales throw it up after eating sea plants because their intestines are irritated. Then they vomit this gift, looking for the lucky one who finds it. Praise be to God, it is a perfume that does not dissolve with water, but rather remains consistent as it was where I found it. At that moment, I wanted to kiss the grandiose whale, which gave me more then I wished, and I knew then why God had entrusted to him one of his honorable prophets to keep him in his great belly." "They will work on the ambergris mass after I sell it until, after combining it with additional substances, it produces a scented diluted liquid. It will then be distributed among dozens of bottles to be used by beautiful women. I will sell it in Sur after we return. I know the man who trades in it. I will go to his place." Farhan told me that his heart almost stopped when he found the ambergris and remembered that there were dozens of other people on board the ship. He feared that a pungent odor of ambergris would quickly ratting itself if he did not act well. He was asking himself, "What if the quarrelsome sailors knew about it?" They will certainly not be going to grant him anything. What is found in the sea must be shared by everyone, that is the prevailing custom. He looked at me grimly, that he did not remember that anyone had shared anything with him before. Then he asked me a confused question. "Why should the customs be applied only to me, Aqeel?" I did not know how to answer. I am not a sailor and I do not know what their customs are. Then he added, "The ambergris is for me and my children only. How can this opportunity be repeated? Does the sea throw us its treasures every day?"

After he said it, he seemed to react sadly. "I will donate some of the money that is left after the workshop opening. I will give it to you, Aqeel."

I congratulated him on what he had obtained and told him, "We do not eat charity, for it is forbidden to the nobles." Then I asked him how he managed to raise it from the sea without anyone seeing it?

"That was my misfortune, I could not have skipped the

sailors to let the stairs down, and if I had thrown myself into the sea, I would make a big scene? Nothing is perfect as they say, I don't know why beautiful things are not always complete? It is the eternal curse of fate; it is never complete. I quietly dangled on the anchor rope, carrying the quilt with me, and wrapped the piece of ambergris with it. I climbed up the same road, hoping that no one would notice me.

"I went down quietly till I was close to three meters from reaching it. Its smell grew stronger, so I didn't know how to hide it from them. I spoke to it like a lover; 'I know you are of a huge aroma, my sweet, please at least lighten your scent now, come to me, precious ball.' I searched well around it, that I might have seen a small piece separated from it, that would add an amount to what I shall earn from this great treasure. My heart was beating so hard that you could hear it from far; or so I thought. I was afraid that my heart would expose me before its smell. I asked God for help in climbing the thick rope. It would not have been that hard had it not been for the oil that filled my hands as a result of touching my precious treasure. It was as if ages passed till I was able to reach my box and hide my little treasure without anyone noticing me."

I congratulated him again with all my heart for his amazing luck, and I congratulated myself on my patience over hearing his long story, and then asked his permission to leave. He followed me saying, "But you accept the gift, right?" I smiled at him and I felt that it is more of a token to keep his secret rather than a gift.

I had insomnia that I was not used to on the night of the second day of sailing from Zanzibar. I looked around me and the rudder was looking at his compass holding the path set for him, and the ship's captain was lying on the surface near him. His eyes were present on the path linked to a star above his head, watching it. He opened his eyes to follow it. Even if his body sometimes fell asleep, a cry from him is enough to shake the body of the rudder and everyone who heard it when the ship drifted off the path set for it. I heard that cry twice.

Three children, the eldest of whom was the son of the ship captain, and two of his relatives were in deep sleep. They were brought to be prepared to be the ship captains. After several years, they would become stronger and lead the ships of their families. Children grow up prematurely in Sur.

All the ship captains in Sur have been through this. They learn everything about the ship, the names of the winds, their directions, and their effect on the sails, they take the reading of the compass, Al Kamal, and they identify directions at sea. During the day, they are assigned to help the crew of the ship in simple works in addition to reciting the Holy Quran and poems. At the end of the day, after eating their early dinner, the youngsters sleep deeply and wake up at the call for dawn prayer, ready for another day.

On the morning of the third day, the sailors adjusted the position of the sails pushed by the winds of Al-Kos to cope with the change in the direction of the wind. Then, the ship's captain chose an appropriate sea-lane to achieve maximum benefit so that the ship did not open a path at a great angle so that we don't move away from the end point a lot. It seems that my stay for three months made me learn many things involuntarily.

The captain of the ship called Jamal chose a very far sea-lane to the right so as not to be affected by the waves and then rise at full speed to the end point, taking advantage of the force of the wind. That is their plan then; a smart plan that Captain Nasser knew no doubt, but he preferred to win the hard way as usual.

He was ordering to run the engine at full speed when the wind was low, although that was dangerous because of a previous problem in the engine. The race went on for several days during which the ship Jamal had disappeared in the direction they chose. I was very worried that we might lose.

10th of Dhu'l-Qi'dah 1378 AH (May 17, 1959)

We proceeded with our travels for ten days, unaware of where the competitor is. We were advancing well and even suppressed some of the ships that went ahead of us by a full day.

We approached Ras Hafun in Somalia, unable to make out where the competing ship is. However, we were brought back to life as one of the sailors shouted that they lagged behind by several miles. They were looming near from the horizon aided by the strong push of the air; their big sail appeared full of it.

The marching of our drums quickly became louder and the sailors went berserk dancing. For the first time I saw Captain Nasser joining the Swahili singing ring the sailors made and in their dancing. And unlike I have expected, he was moving very lightly, in perfect sync with the other sailors with delight lighting up his face. We were all happy about this. We made it with them a few miles behind us, and I listened to the singing that I could not understand.

"Lebeni maji manawi, Mokonw sheka sheka."

Riled up by their anger and speed they draw dangerously close to us while our crew picked up the pace dancing, singing, and clapping to irritate them further. The ship's captain yelled at them, "Add sails of your mothers' gowns to the sail if you want to suppress Samha."

One can only wonder how 'Ibn al-Tair' felt then but I can

imagine that he was certainly unhappy. I seldom heard the ship's captain raise his voice. He was naturally calm with several outbursts from time to time for reasons I was completely unaware of. I thanked God that our ship won, as I was agitated in the long race consumed by my loyalty to Samha and its crew. I also did not know what would be the ship's captain reaction if we lost the race. Everything was to be expected as Ali has repeatedly told me. I asked Ali later about the threat the ship's captain threw at everyone and he smiled and told me that he was confident in Samha and her crew despite his concern over the engine; his answer did not bring me any relief.

After the race, the ship Jamal headed into Hafun port while a Suri ship called al-Naif approached us. The weather was refreshing and the sky was clear; the ship captain called the captain of al-Naif, Ibn al-Khayal, and asked him to provide us with water due to how much was consumed throughout the previous few days by the passengers. Al-Naif had no passengers boarding it and he had more than enough water to spare some to Samah, which was full of passengers and we have not made any trips to fetch water from any port.

After completing the loading process, the ship's captain of al-Naif wanted to pull back quickly. However, Captain Nasser asked for 'Sinyyar' or to be accompanied in the path. The engine has been a cause of obsession for the ship captain, as Ali told me, despite the fact that it was fully maintained in India. I felt that the request for companionship had caused Ibn Al-Khayal severe embarrassment, as if he had expected it, but he would not have to reject an old custom. Otherwise, it would be a precedent among the ship captains.

Al-Naif had to reduce its speed to keep pace with us, a

gracious and slow path due to the weak engine, and the sails were not useful because the winds faded after crossing the Horn of Africa. Our journey lasted for several days until we arrived at Al-Sawda Island from the Omani islands of Kuriya Moriya. The ship's captain was worried about something that I could not figure out. I attributed it to the weak engine. The crew was working tirelessly in the daily sea chores, and the travelers killed time with conversations. The ship's captain continues to train his son, who is not over thirteen, to use al-Kamal on a daily basis. I recited Juz Amma to him as requested by the ship captain and whenever I had available time I used to sit with Obaid and Farhan to chat.

15th of Dhu'l-Qi'dah1378 AH (May 22, 1959)

After passing the island of 'Socotra,' the sea changed dramatically. Winds of different speeds and long slow-moving waves, a storm was occurring far away according to the ship captain's expression. During this time, we were unable to gather and talk as usual. The sailors were busy with their daily work, and some travelers were emptying their stomachs. The general atmosphere was not comfortable at all. The past days disturbed us. The weather was unprecedentedly turbulent, foretelling of a big and close event at the same time. The matter was made worse by the endless numbers of long waves that hampered our journey with its constant movement under the ship; a clear sign of what will happen next. That was what I told myself before being slapped by a sudden gust of wind that took me out of this self-talk. After that, I was sure that this disturbance would have consequences. I was reviewing Surat An-Naza'at with the ship captain's son but then I halted reading and asked him to lay down on a bed near his father's wardrobe. He seemed uneasy and my stomach was just uneasy but I tried to brave it as much as possible.

Abruptly the winds settled down before we reached Kuriya Muriya Islands and that cheered up passengers and the new sailors, but the senior sailors turned uneasily silent. This unforeseen quiet is only a warning of something worse and more dangerous nearing, as Ali has told me. This is how the sea taught them the hard way, and the practical experience they paid for with some of their friends who previously settled down in its depths.

The presence of a small propulsion engine in the ship was a reason for reassurance as it can push the ship, even slowly, out of the circle of danger that was approaching without the need to wait for a miracle to push the ship forward; given that it is not possible to raise any kind of sails at the time of storms.

The anxiety returned when the change began quickly on the surface of the water. A hot, dry wind flared at us for two hours from the direction of the land. The direction of the wind changed after that again to come rushing from the sea. He was then certain that the storm would return more strongly this time as the waves, pushed by these increasing winds, accelerated. I was with the ship captain's son when Ali approached to ask me about something that occurred to him. He found the ship captain studying the Almanac pointing with his fingers at one word among many that were listed one under another in a list written in red, each corresponding to a specific number.

"It is Darbat al'Iiklil that I expected after we have sailed late. It looks like it's eleven days ahead of schedule, which will inevitably put us in the midst of the storm."

"What to do then? There is no shelter nearby and the ship is overcrowded with goods and passengers."

"No need to worry. Samha will be able to handle it, but the ship must be well prepared to withstand what we will face, which will be different from what we have already encountered. This storm is building its waves faster than anything I've seen before, and we won't have much time to do after that."

Ali understood what to do with a mere nod, and I had doubts about whether it is just a storm. The ship captain's tone betrayed his anxiety despite how confident he sounded. Ali started assigning work to the men. They started tightening the ropes on the loose goods on the deck well, retying what had already been tied tightly ensuring its stability, and they did it all while singing and chanting as usual.

He distributed the crew of sailors according to their skills; a division that no one else but him knows. This is evident in assigning a specific person to work that requires special skills, such as preparing sails, replacing some ropes with other ropes, tying certain knots on the girders, or preparing pulleys for lifting or lowering weights. While some sailors were ordered to carry out individual work that requires great physical strength, as for teamwork, everyone participated in it and no one was excused from working with the rest of the crew. They obeyed him without a question, and the ship's captain undoubtedly did well choosing Ali to be the second man in Samha.

The passengers were anxious as they saw the weather changing and how the sailors moved everywhere. Most of them resided within the inner regions of Oman and were unaccustomed to the inconstancy of the sea except through few incidents such as what happened three days ago. I have not seen the frantic movement of the sailors engaged in preparing the ship so quickly and seriously since the beginning of our voyage. Despite everything, the sailors singing was reassuring for them. It raises a legitimate concern in the mind as the state of the sea changed so quickly. "Is fate preparing anything for us? We have heard a lot about the horrors of the seas that the sailors witness, so will we see it firsthand?"

The women and children were ushered to the lower chamber, which is prepared for them, while men gathered in small circles in the middle of the ship as it started rocking left and right due to the waves hitting it. The ship's captain stood watching the black clouds that were rushing toward us, pushed by strong boisterous winds that sounded like the howling of wolves or the wailing of women.

16th of Dhu'l-Qi'dah 1378 AH (May 23, 1959)

Heavier than Samha, I had a day like never before. I lost sense of my balance and I tried to escape by sleeping after I suffered from nausea. I tried to throw up but could not, which put me in an even worse mood that stayed through the rampage of the waves, and the swinging of the ship left and right, without actually advancing but a few meters forward each hour.

We were unable to pray together; how will we be able to do so and we are not able to queue beside each other? Some of them used to perform ablution quickly and head as agreed to the west to pray in order to finish the prayers and shorten them quickly, to begin their suffering with the waves again afterward. I saw the cook struggling that day to prepare a large meal sufficient for the crew and travelers. He threw it into the sea because they did not want to eat. I saw plates full of rice that the sailors took to the lower room for the women and children and returned them as they were; no doubt that they suffered more than us in that bleak prison.

The night crawled murky black and with fearsome solemnity. The sound of the waves hitting the sides of Samha was like the sound of drumbeats, crashing like a big drum, and the clouds gathered above us to increase the gloominess of the night even more. Those walking on the deck were unable to escape bruises and standing on a steady ground seemed like a dream at the time. According to the ship's captain, the tornado was approaching rapidly. He told me that it is Darbat al'Iiklil that comes at that time of the year. That was the cause of his concern that I did not seem to understand. How alluring is the sea when calm and how dreadful it is when angry.

I heard a shriek of hurt coming from al-Siridan, where the dinner is cooked inside a big wooden box, on the deck of the wooden ship. I rushed to get there and many sailors have also gathered around the poor cook whose hand skin is deep red as a bowl of boiling water fell on it. The sailors tried to treat him as they could, and I saw one of them open a can of tomatoes and wipe it on his hand and then wrap a piece of cloth on it, I didn't know if it was a suitable treatment but the cook accepted it.

17th of Dhu'l-Qi'dah 1378 AH (May 24, 1959)

Midday, as we were moving incredibly slowly near Ghubat Ash Shuwaymiyyah, the weather has changed to waves of the kind that sailors were used to. As we passed Khuriya Muriya Islands, a state of poor visibility prevailed around the place that made us not see al-Naif when it was only one mile away from us. The sky was not completely overcast with clouds, but the density of cumulus clouds that seemed to carry a lot of water had taken over the western side where any trace of the sun had disappeared. Its weak threads could not penetrate the density of the clouds accumulated on top of each other.

The clouds accelerated until they covered the entire area. This spot is called al-Raas al-Ahmar, in relation to a completely smooth mountain that extended to the sky as if it is a genie that you can only see the middle part of with his feet in the sea and his head touching the clouds.

The ship's captain asked me to sit near his son, as he was busy managing the ship in this dire situation. He did not want to send him to the room where the women and children are. He wanted him to get used to seeing waves and the choppy conditions of the sea, and I pitied the boy who did not show any fear.

Ali asked the ship's captain, "What do you think of the situation?"

The dark caused by the thick clouds preceded the

nightfall. Waves were billowing and Samha was moving steadily. The waves' shifting directions and their approach to the shore are what I fear, as we were not that far away from this seemingly endless mountain range.

The waves were building up slowly and the dense clouds took over the whole sky. Samha was like a feather in the wind and could only obey the increasing waves. If it was not for her remaining on the set path, I would have thought that we lost control over the ship and were swallowed by uncharted darkness.

A far squall arose from the sea trying to reach the sky on the right of the ship and it was summoning its might from the warm seawater. It appeared to us, as we looked at it, that it was increasing its strength in a direct direction to land intersecting with the intended path of the ship. The point of the clash was after two hours according to the ship captain's estimation who did not have many options but to act on it.

The force of the waves weakened the efficiency of the engine due to the rise of the stern of the ship sometimes, and the front of it at other times, which slowed the rotation of the propeller. Relentless, the ship's captain insisted to keep it running since the sails were useless with all of these raging winds and waves as well as to maintain a straight path avoiding nearing the shores and intersecting with the waves on an acute angle at the same time to intake some of the effects of the front and side waves. This will lessen the burden on the passengers and the ship altogether, and it somewhat worked.

An hour later, the waves were still striking the ship's deck at the front and escaped from its rear. The situation turned worse as the winds picked up their power and started moving the goods fixed on the ship's deck after some ropes were cut due to the ship's violent movement and the waves continuous collision with it.

We remained in the same state until the afternoon of the second day when the ship's captain found a spot suitable for throwing the hook on, which did not provide much protection, but it was better than fighting the waves anyway, or so we thought at least. Samha approached al-Naif to discuss the situation and the two men agreed on casting anchors in this exact spot until the morning as the waves were not enough source for our suffering, the sky pouring with heavy rain, and only God knew how we were.

Reclining on the water tank, I saw Farhan sitting, indifferent to what is happening around him. Does getting accustomed to it make one this senseless? He nodded to me to sit and to my bewilderment, he started reciting verses from a poem that he mentioned was by Saeed bin Wazir that perfectly described what we were living at the moment:

"One time, the sea showed his claws In fury, he raised the
wave
The rain poured, seemingly endless Too bleak for a one to
brave
The heavy rain left nowhere on the deck dry Enemies
separated and broke free
The sun is gone, the moon is a far cry Four nights followed
the day
Dhuhr and Asr are too alike,
A later prayer is all that we can give
We fear for the mast with each thunder strike Aimed to take
it down, to desperately live The waves had another say on
that

Stricken with doom, heavy with sorrow Standing on the
death's doormat
The mast was cut and laid low."

Barely an hour passed until Ibn Wazir's poem came true with all of its terrifying details as if Farhan was seeing the unseen from a transparent curtain. Unannounced, Samha moved with its anchor, which soon broke off due to the intensifying waves. As a result, the ship moved in a frenzy as the engine had been turned off. The engine operator tried to reach it in vain and some sailors ran to turn it on. Ali encouraged them tirelessly until one of them managed to turn it on, and the ship took a straight path for a few moments until the engine made a cacophonous sound that soon died out, and the ship became like a worn-out rag in which the waves moved as it pleased.

Seawater and rain were entering the inside of the ship in large quantities after the deck covers broke off, and some of them fell into the sea due to the violent movement of the waves.

"Cut the mast immediately!" "Cut the mast immediately!"

The ship's captain commanded in an attempt to restore the balance of the ship after the seawater and the flowing rainwater disturbed it. The mast weight was a burden on the ship making her lean in one direction. Farhan and three senior sailors looked for the saw and finding it, in those circumstances, appeared to be more burdensome than the task of cutting the mast which would end disastrously if they weren't so careful about it.

In no way was it an easy task. The waves spared them no time to carry out the task as necessary. The dark fell and they did not have enough lights. They managed to cut off two-thirds of the base, but the two-grip saw escaped them after a slap from a sweeping wave and turbulent movement from the ship and it flew off, injuring one of the sailors severely in his right leg.

Farhan decided that the priority at that moment was to complete the cutting of the mast, rather than save the poor sailor who screamed in pain, writhing, and blood flowing profusely. "Tie up your wound with your clothes until we finish," Farhan said as they completed cutting the mast. I was watching the sailor writhing in pain and his blood mixed with seawater, and I had nothing that I can do for him as moving near was dangerous with the ship swaying violently.

Before finishing the cutting of the mast, Farhan ordered the sailors with him to grab the rope controlling the mast to direct its fall, but a very large wave had lifted the ship high and threw it on the water again, causing the upper part of the mast to break and most of it fell without warning into the sea. The lower third smashed with tremendous force on the deck, destroying the ship's right side greatly, crushing at the same time the body of the injured sailor; the sound of his ribs breaking blended with the sound of the wind and the voices of the sailors who were shocked by the blow that turned him into a torn corpse.

We were all horrified as we witnessed it. I was terrified and sat where I had stood. The sailors tried to pull themselves together as the ship's captain stepped in trying to push what was left of the mast into the sea while Ali took an ax cutting off the remaining ropes that kept the mast on the ship's deck. The sailors and some of the passengers pushed the heavy mast into the sea until the ship was lighter, while some of them took care of collecting the scattering remains of their friend, the dead sailor, and wrapped him in a wet blanket for now.

The sky suddenly split with a bolt of lightning that almost blinded everyone who saw it, turning darkness into light that was enough to see what was happening around us. As we were sure that we were about to enter the circle of a deadly hurricane during the next hour, everything was prepared for that.

The lighting was followed by a great flow of thunder, and soon after the sky started pouring even more intensely than before. After a couple of hours of heavy rain, Samha started swinging heavily due to the water flowing into it, moving left and right, steering against the movement of the waves, which paralyzed it completely, making it dead in its track.

The rest of the sailors and passengers were instructed to remove the water seeping into the inside of the ship using buckets. We quickly lined up to speed up the process, which seemed impossible, as the amount of water leaking was large, and its movement with the waves worsened the ship's balance. The worst of all was the vicious smell of fish oil that emitted strongly from the boards of the inside of the ship and which are not exposed to the sun so the smell subsides.

An old man, a blind, a hunchback, a boy, and a Bedouin lined up near me, everyone doing their best to save the ship. I could only stay for a few minutes and I quickly went out to breathe fresh air after I was so nauseous that I almost fell unconscious. This trip showed me my fragility in the calamities. I headed to where the ship's captain and Ali were consulting.

"Is it the end?" the coxswain asked the ship captain.

"It is our fate; one cannot know their destiny. We have no

sails nor an anchor, and the engine stopped working. Our last hope is that the engine starts to work again or we are fall to our doom. Do you see our Sinyyar?"

"They seem to be in a similar situation to ours, though far from us I caught a glimpse of their ship swinging wildly and their crew all running toward their deck at the time of lightning."

"How are the women and children?"

"May God help them. Some of them died before they knew it and some of them had their rooms filled with water and found no way out of it. We at least are able to see death approaching us and we are able to breathe fresh air, while they are stuck in that dark cell filled to the brim with people with no air to breathe. They might find themselves falling into the depths of the sea, unable to escape death."

These words added a grim dark cloud above the ship captain's head. No amount of water splashing from the rain and waves could be able to wash it away. He felt great distress and deep sadness for the fate that these poor people might meet if the situation continued in this way without change. Ali suggested unloading some of the cargo.

"Yes, do that to an appropriate extent and remember that they are our responsibility."

"Are the souls you are holding in your hands not your responsibility as well? Were you not able to buy a new engine in India five months ago, fully aware of the deficiency of this one when you know that it always broke down? Who will be held accountable for the souls on the ship right now? Is there an end to your stubbornness?"

"I will be responsible for everything, Ali. I am the ship's captain or did you forget that? It seems like the sailor's death affected you greatly. Do you think a new engine will do much difference in the tornado we are facing? Since when are you shaken by the storms and tornados? Is it the desire to live reigniting within you now at the sight of the thunder, rain, and wind? Was it not you who always stated that living past fifty years is a luxury?"

"Did we sail to kill ourselves and everyone with us? If we lived enough, then what about the boys and girls that did not get to live it yet? Who are we to decide who dies and lives among people?"

"Those who face the sea cannot be scared of the splashing of the waves Ali. It is not us who will decide how their lives will end."

"It is all fate."

"We will do our best to escape the current situation."

This was the first time that I saw Ali arguing back against the ship's captain. The first time since the beginning of our journey that I have seen uncertainty flashing in the ship captain's eyes. Since when did this stubborn old man that experienced the seas for over fifty years is shaken?

It is the will of God first and foremost, then it is the forces of nature, murderous and merciless toward anyone. If the time comes, ironically, and my end is on my first journey, there are only days left until our arrival, and the land is not far away, but how to reach it? Oh, how miserable are these last moments.

The sailors threw the cargo belonging to Obeid first. It was an impediment to move freely on the surface. I looked at poor Obeid; the miserable man seemed to be stuck near me. He did not know what to do and he could not throw his future into the sea. He sees his capital and all his wishes and dreams cast into the sea in front of his eyes, and he has nothing of the matter. I caught a smile from another sailor as he threw that shipment, he did it with joy. Whenever the sailor threw, Obeid was getting gloomier in the darkness of an unforgiving sky; he bid his yearning for a better life farewell.

With every time the sailor throws something, Obeid saw his father juggling coffee cups. These images are fading from his memory, which seemed heavier than Samha. With every piece thrown, Obeid wondered if there is any point in staying on the deck of Samha; the one that drowned his hopes and made everyone relish in his pain. How would the fugitive return empty-handed? At this moment, Obeid was heavier than Samha itself; perhaps if he was thrown off the ship into the sea the curse hunting it would escape it as well.

The wind speed doubled, determining our direction became impossible. We knew for sure that we had entered the eye of the hurricane. We felt a clear change in the movement of the wind direction, with great pressure at the same time, and a rapid change in the temperature. Suddenly, another strong glimmer appeared that showed the whole picture to us, then we could only repeat al-Hawqala.

"May God have mercy on us," came a weak feminine voice that emphasized fear with each letter; the lady could not stay put in the women's chamber.

"Whose voice is that?" asked the ship's captain.

"Mariam, Juma's wife. The cover protecting the women's chamber was yanked and a lot of water leaked inside. It is indescribably turbulence inside, do something for the poor souls that are rendered helpless in this situation. It is extremely tiring and everyone is cramped. Women are holding the children up afraid they will drown and the water is almost filling the lower chamber to the brim."

We could not find a response to this disastrous situation that fell upon us. We could not see any sailors, all of them busy at these moments.

"Hold on tight." The words slipped out with difficulty. He then continued, "O God if that was the end, make it come quick."

Those were his other words, after which a flash cutting through the sky lasted a few seconds forming what looked like the number seven as if a hand was extended to heaven in response to that prayer.

Helpless as a result of what was happening, I sat alone and wet, so I began to recite Ayatul-kursi and some prayers hoping that God would save us from what had befallen us. I felt a rough hand patting my shoulder, and I looked and saw Farhan standing above my head. He sat next to me. "I must tell you something, Aqeel," he said. Farhan was unlike anything I have ever seen him.

"I will not make use of the piece of Amber, Aqeel." "How is that and you have it with you?"

"It's a cursed piece. I cursed it repeatedly after its voice bothered me before I knew what it was. Nobody benefits from something cursed at all. I will not leave it, but it will not benefit me. I do not doubt that our end in this journey, we will die by drowning. Oh, Aqeel, do you not see how the waves grow and how strong is this wind? It is the reason we are in. It is cursed, there is no doubt about that, but I will not throw away this treasure of mine until I am freed from its curse. I will die while I hold it."

Then he laughed loudly, saying, "O how wretched is this life; it extends its hand to you graciously, and when your hands touch its gifts, it snatches the dearest things you have."

His words put fear in my heart. He seemed certain of what he is saying. I sought refuge in God from these insinuations, and I read something from the dhikr.

After four consecutive hours, I was exhausted by the waves, and I had no energy left in me to bear this situation anymore. I saw the poor Jawad struggling after he emptied his stomach at the side of the ship, he then sat extending his legs in front of him. He was suffering from colic and fluctuations in his intestines, like some travelers who are not accustomed to riding the sea. I gave him some water, then he took half a lemon out of his pocket and started sucking it hoping that it will help him regain some of the balance he lost. I sat next to him in silence and he then looked at me, his inside calm. "Do not you see, Aqeel? My fate has been connected to the ship's captain for years," he said. "It is an inescapable fate," he continued.

Dawn of 18 of Dhu'l-Qi'dah 1378 AH (Dawn – May 25, 1959)

The crew of Al-Naif noticed us from a distance, so they knew what happened. They came toward us trying to pull Samha. It was not easy to approach, no one wanted to get involved in getting too close to a ship whose movement is unpredictable. Our crew tried to throw the towing rope to them several times, but the strong winds prevented that.

The rope is heavy and cannot be thrown easily. It has been attached at its end to another light rope that is easy to throw to the other ship, attaching it to an iron weight so that the wind would not throw it away. The method succeeded after two attempts and the crew of Al-Naif pulled the smaller rope followed by the thick rope that sank in the sea. After moving for five meters, a big wave cut off the rope pulled by the crew of Al-Naif.

Attempts to connect the rope in this way seemed impossible. Someone suggested lowering the small boat quickly on Samha's starboard where a somewhat quiet area was formed due to the presence of Al-Naif behind Samha which formed a temporary dam for the waves that were coming from behind. The small boat was lowered very quickly and then a net of fibers was cast over it and used as a temporary stair. Ali ordered one of the sailors to go down quickly then he shouted, "Let someone else go down and help him to hold the rope."

I was the closest of them to the stairs. I got terrified of the idea, although I am not forced to do it, but due to the acute situation, someone had to volunteer quickly. I looked around me and my eyes met the eyes of the captain; he nodded to me to go. I found myself climbing down the net used as stairs hanging half way between Samha and the lifeboat. The huge waves were raising and lowering the lifeboat as I was trying my best not to fall into the sea, and was able to make it at last with a strong fall in the boat.

The other sailor was doing everything to keep the boat close to the ship, so that I could get in it. The sailors threw us the thick rope and I struggled to catch it after I got on the boat. Samha was rising and falling with great force, causing side waves that were worse than the hurricane waves because it was close to us. The situation became dangerous, especially after a terrifying gap appeared beneath Samha due to its repeated rising and falling back to the water again. If we were swept by the waves to that area beneath the ship, we would be crushed in no time under the gigantic wooden structure.

Samha moved away from us and we started striving in the midst of our small boat which would sink at any moment. The heavy rope following Samha would slip from me had it not been for the sailor warning me to leave it. Only half a meter remained to pull me with it into the sea to where there is no return. The rope broke completely and it sank into the sea. Samha continued to move away without guidance. A large wave nearly capsized the boat. We were completely immersed in the sea like wild horses galloping in every direction. Many questions ran in my head. "What am I doing in the middle of this clogged sea? What made me get into the boat? Is this my end? How will I go back to Samha again?"

What I heard, from the description of the waves, was something completely different from what I saw. I was overwhelmed by a state of complete panic. Mountains of huge waves advanced toward us from the starboard. We became open to them because of the space made when Samha moved away from us. A real death that only a piece of wood called a boat separated me from, then a tough wave hit me afterwards. I knew that it was the end.

For a moment, I became like someone who drowned in a well and then came out to breathe. I didn't know what happened to me. I lost directions and forgot even where I was. I heard the voices of the sailors of Al-Naif calling us from behind. Their call brought hope back to me. Someone called me, "Come on, get in quickly." I turned and saw that Al-Naif had shaded us, as if it were a mountain shaking left and right, and the sailors had lowered a net of ropes so that we could climb upwards.

I struggled to catch the net which was half a meter above me. I was helped by a wave that tossed the boat up and climbed so quickly that when I reached the surface I felt numbness in my right hand. One of the sailors gave me his hand which was like a passage to a new life. My friend, who also seemed tired, followed me. He let go of the paddle and grabbed the end of the net trying to get up, with the sailors urging him to do so.

With both hands, the sailor held the net but the ship's turbulent movement kept his body in the air. While the boat slipped away from beneath him, he tried to reach his legs to the hull of the ship to help him go up but he couldn't. The sailors pulled the net to raise him quickly and his body came close to the surface. Before the sailors could get hold of him,

Al-Naif moved violently after descending from a great wave. The poor sailor's hands escaped and he fell under the huge hull of the ship.

One of the sailors wanted to jump to save him, but they stopped him due to the seriousness of the situation. The body of the sailor did not appear after that. We looked in every direction, the boat drifted away from Al-Naif, and the body of the sailor lay under the ship, which continued to rise and fall strongly because the engine was stopped. Al-Naif moved a little to search for the sailor but it was pointless. We could not see a trace of him after that. There is no doubt that death was hovering over our heads like an eagle over its prey that day.

This is how I became part of the crew of another ship. I see my friends moving away, not knowing my end or theirs, and whoever the poor sailor I was with a while ago was swallowed by the sea; he was no more than twenty years old. I am almost sure that the body of the ship smashed his thin body. If he was alive, he would have swum as the Suri sailors are all good swimmers. It was getting darker, and the sea became darker, and you could only hear the roaring of the waves, the clanking of the ship's timbers, and the incessant shouts of the sailors.

Night of 18 Dhu'l-Qi'dah 1378 AH (Night – May 25, 1959)

Like a wet bird, I sat on the stern of Al-Naif. Watching Samha and those I traveled with there, I refused to join the rest of the passengers. They respected my desire, the scene of parting from a ship I spent three months on with the best sailors I encountered. Samha was heading toward the mountain without deviating. She is not bound by a wave or a hurricane. You think of her as if she was moving like a bride in full adornment that is wed to death.

What a finely drawn ending. Are the trajectories of our lives written like this? What is Farhan the carpenter telling himself there? Is Ali still running among his sailors, encouraging and urging them to finish work quickly? Were the features of the ship captain finally changed to legitimate confusion after all that unshaken confidence? Will Jawad die in the sea after God saved him from death in the desert?

Successive thunderbolts of lightning struck the horizon, and then the night became day after that, and despite our distance from Samha, its personnel seemed clearer to me. I saw a group of travelers crumpled as if they were a large body squatting, a sailor running fast, and others struggling to throw boxes from the roof into the sea, the young son of the ship captain clinging to his father.

The rain became more and more abundant as if the sky had become a giant water bladder that was cut in length with a sharp dagger, the wind performing the dance of madness without stopping and its voices are the howling of old women after a great pandemic. Samha is on its way to its inevitable doom as the mountain seemed to me a giant death with its arms outstretched, preparing to embrace them.

A great ark flowing in greater waves, the first time I saw Samha sailing away while I was not on it, I saw her huge size, luxurious in construction, coherent in structure. As if I was watching her for the first time, sailing with determination to a written goal, penetrating waves and riding others, full of people and struggling for life in the midst of a dark sea.

Samha was covered by a great wave that did not appear after. I knew that this was her end, if it were not for the emergence of its front significantly higher after a while, after which a rear wave ran along and pushed her forward. Even if she was at the top of it, she completed the ascent. She seemed to me as a bride ascending the stairs, leaving her old world behind, it struggled up with determination, and then the place was completely darkened.

Her inevitable end has been hidden from me, elegant and rebellious even in her absence, after which the intensity of the waves subsided and I felt the stillness of the wind. Its voice changed to a sharp sob and I felt complete numbness in my body. A long silence, I was shambling, that was the last time for me to see her.

Dawn of 19 of Dhu'l-Qi'dah 1378 AH (Dawn – May 26, 1959)

The matter reached the most severe for us in Al-Naif. The hurricane had passed, and left us the waves and the winds that came back to us which doubled the strength and violence of the waves. It was too dark and you could only hear the ship crashing to the surface of the sea after the waves raised it high and descended it violently. The whole crew on the deck is wet and clinging to the closest piece of the ship.

Two hours after dawn, the wind subsided and the waves calmed down in a way that we were able to gather ourselves. The sunshine appeared to us after an absence; the clouds preceded it moving away to the west; the rain stopped. The ship's captain of Al-Naif decided to continue sailing. The beach was close to us and we were looking in every direction. Perhaps we would see a trace of Samha and her crew, but to no avail. When we approached the coast, the ship's captain ordered to lower the Bild – a rope with a piece of lead at its end and with signs on the rope to indicate the depth of the sea. He found that it is eleven Baa'a in depth. The captain continued sailing reassuringly in the same direction. It was only few moments until the ship shook after a terrible collision force that pushed us forward and stopped Al-Naif in its place.

A sailor shouted to the ship's captain. We hit a sand ridge from the front. It was in front of us submerged under the water only two meters away. Al-Naif stood still in its place perfectly and it was only a matter of minutes until Al-Naif seemed to tilt toward the right. The crew lowered the ship's boats very quickly and we took what we could of water and dates. Al-Naifs tilting increased rapidly posing a danger to the crew. Al-Naif was not carrying any passengers because it did not set off from Zanzibar, that big port, but rather sailed from the port of Ngomeini.

The sailors jumped, swimming toward the nearby shore, and I stood hesitant. To be from Sur and don't know how to swim, that is a shame. A clever sailor beheld me, standing near the ship's boat, and asked me to wait so I can help to lower the boat. His intelligence was a lifeline to me from drowning and embarrassment. Who can bear both shame and drowning together?

We stood on the shore exhausted and watching Al-Naif, tilted with water seeping into it from all sides. We could not believe that we were still alive. I threw myself on the sand, exhausted, and so did most of the crew. Ibn Al-Khayal was standing looking sullenly at his ship, which cracked hard by the shock of the sand ridge. He told us, looking at his ship:

"The hurricane could not drown us, so we were drowned by a mass of sand hiding under the sea. We spent half a day on the beach gathering our scattered selves and our exhausted bodies. Most of our talk was about our Sinyyar, which we know nothing about. Ibn Al-Khayal was certain of their doom.

I heard him telling one of the sailors that Samha moved toward the mountain after its anchor was separated and the engine broke down. Samha crew had nothing to do. The mountain was meters away from where they separated from us and the waves were pushing them to it; there was no way to change their collision with it.

A lump caused by the loss of Samha, I didn't tell anyone what I heard. What happened in that dark room with little air and full of children and women? Death must have been wandering there, it was hell, I couldn't imagine the situation, my breath is racing and I was heartbroken to remember them, and I am here on dry safe land. What tragedy happened to them?

Have all those sailors and men gone? Were the dreams of the girls ready to marry their relatives in Oman dashed for fear of mixing Arab blood in Zanzibar? Did the children sleep that night at the bottom of the sea? Did I lose Ali and Farhan forever? Had the ship's captain, that honorable man, left us? Any news will reach Sur in a few days? Undoubtedly, death has a sharp sword that squanders hopes, erases dreams and wishes.

Half a day passed in which we were miserable, wet, lost, and alone in a barren, poor, and uninhabited environment, we did not know what to do until a group of Bedouins passed by. They asked us for food, and we didn't have any. When they realized our situation, they decided to leave. We reminded them of the inherent customs, and that their duty is not to leave us in that miserable situation and we do not know where we are. We asked them to take us to the nearest town.

We were not a great prize for the Bedouins, who agreed with heavy hearts. The features of indigence are visible on their faces also. We walked behind them, sixteen men for seven hours straight, until the Bedouins suggested that we rest a little. We shared what we had of small provisions with them.

We continued the walk until sunset and then laid down with the sky above us and our hands folded as pillows under our heads.

The next morning, we climbed a high mountain road; two hours to its summit and it was flat from the top like a vast sea. We continued walking until noon provided with two water bottles, a few dates, and a jar of dried meat which the coxswain of Al-Naif carried with him. It was a great help to us, with his keenness to distribute small portions to everyone every six hours.

The fresh air after the hurricane was a source of happiness despite the pain in the heart. Perhaps the real reason for our happiness is our survival. Feelings mix between sadness for loss, and joy for survival; we don't know which one is more honest. The rain stopped but some clouds still remain. I see misery in the sailors face. There is no doubt that the sadness of the ship's captain of Al-Naif is deeper.

In the afternoon, we approached a camp for one of the companies working in paving roads. They saw us from the top of the mountain while they were preparing for prayer. They were surprised seeing us rushing toward them, pushed by the steep mountainside. They left their prayer running toward their guns. The political conditions are very turbulent in Oman, and the conflicts of some tribes continue. Hunger is rampant and security is missing; their caution was justified.

The company's Omani guards pointed their weapons at us, asking us to stop where we were. Two men came and the Bedouins and Ibn al-Khayal headed toward them. They spoke for a little while then they waved to us to move toward them and we arrived with a great deal of exhaustion and hunger. The men honored us decently in their humble camp. We showered, washed our clothes, and sat for two days in their hospitality after which their cars took us to Thumrait and we stayed there for one night."

22nd Of Dhu'l-Qi'dah 1378 (May 29, 1959)

It took half a day to reach Salalah. The sandy road was affected by the hurricane and we arrived exhausted. The local fishermen in Salalah gave us empty mud storages facing the sea for us to live in. They were used to store the coconuts that are abundant near their homes.

The governor sent us some money that we used to buy what we needed during our stay there while the ship's captain of Al-Naif telegraphed Sur that his crew was fine and would return on the first ship going back to Sur. For long days, we waited for a ship to take us to Sur. The sailing season had closed and the winds of Al-Kos had abated. There was no way but to wait for a wooden boat running with engines, as they are few in the area. We did nothing but kill time by talking to the simple people of the village.

After two weeks of waiting, then a Suri ship has arrived in (Salalah) coming from Yemen carrying a large shipment of coffee; the owner of which was known to the Al-Naif crew. He welcomed us all and we left with him to Sur, thanking the fishermen for their hospitality.

10th of Dhul Hijjah 1378 AH
(June 16, 1959)

At the afternoon of the first day of Eid al-Adha, Sur became clear to us. News had spread about the loss of two Suri ships and several ships from the Gulf and Iran as a result of the hurricane. My parents were happy to see me when I entered the house, and they thanked God for that very much. They wondered how God facilitated my transfer to Al-Naif. Many people visited me congratulating my safety. They were asking about Samha, whom I told them we don't know anything about after its disappearance. I heard after that the house of Ibn Al-Khayal became a destination for people, and Al-Naif crew had to stay in their homes for several days to receive well-wishers for safety and inquirers about Samha of those whose families we left clinging to hope that its crew and those on board will return alive. There are many ships whose crew returned safely after a while from sinking.

Samha's disappearance became a great mystery in Sur, because passengers of other sunken ships were rescued, found their wrecks, or broke and all their passengers were safe as Al-Naif. But Samha, despite the searching by military planes, ships, and local residents, and the many correspondences between the governors of the coastal areas around it, did not show any trace of it and its passengers who exceeded one hundred and forty.

Unhappy Eid days passed that year. We performed its

rituals, but the joy was dissipated from Sur and many of the villages of Oman that lost some of their children. The celebrations stopped, the drums fell silent, and joy disappeared. Hard days during which I watched many of the people of the Samha crew and their sons watching the sea. Perhaps they could see a sail coming dispels the cloud of sadness that hovered over Sur, or of joyful news that restores the soul to the afflicted families.

The notables were following the correspondence, hoping that something new would reach them, but uselessly. Samha refused to express itself. She remained rebel even in her disappearance. Disappeared as one piece, and there was a great silence after that, to the extent that her sailors filled everywhere with noise, with their high energy, celebrations and drums that did not stop, except on the day she said goodbye to us.

A great consolation was held for her crew after a while of her absence. The sinking of Samha was not just the sinking of a passing ship, but it was a sign of closing a bright sailing era that lasted for three centuries, during which a small town turned into a great workshop for shipbuilding and trade, and its men sailed in every direction, forgetting the challenges and hardships in order to have a better life.

Last Scene

Phantoms

Nine months passed since we arrived Sur; the stems of trauma have lessened in people. As for me, I have not even teared up once. I am haunted by their images all the time. I keep hearing their voices, their phantoms reside within me. I see Samha in every sailing ship, I see her sailors in the faces of the Suri sailors. I could not find the ship captain's face among all the ship captains I met daily. I have lost his image; my memory can only conjure a blur of his features.

I was visited by his spirit a month ago, a smiling man not a day past thirty. He stood on the deck of Samha, which seemed bigger and shinier, and it was hanging between the sky and land. He looked at me, nodding his head in a greeting, looked up at the sky, glanced back at his watch, then kept his sight ahead of him. Samha then made her way into the horizon with her sails open like a shooting star on a starry night.

Samha appeared alone in my dream a few days back. She told me that she is now in her eternal resting place, alone, resting after what she faced, like a titan curled up upon himself. Her remains were scattered in the ocean. The bodies of her passengers amalgamated with the salt of the sea, which chops off their bodies every day. She told me that she would rest with them there until she is dissolved into a drop in this great sea, moving freely after, with everyone who she loved near her. There was no way to communicate. It is heartbreaking not being able to hear their talks, to see their glances. She will meet them again when they are finally free of their hardened skeletons on their bodies. She will then call upon their memories; she will restore the sounds of drums that were still echoing despite being dull at the moment. They will swim boundlessly in this immortal sea that witnessed the events crumbling; the one that met with the ships of travelers, merchants, legends, invaders, pirates, and explorers.

She then excused herself, and their phantoms disappeared. I no longer see her among ships, nor her sailors among sailors. Each time I stand in the creek, I smell the Amber faintly so I turn to my right then my left. I look for them all, but they are all gone. Only their phantoms are left reigning heavy in my memory. I comprehended what has happened, filled to the brim with memories, then I was encompassed with sorrow, and my wounds soared with pain.

The End